Blogging 2020

An Essential Guide to Marketing Your Blog and Making Money Online from It, Including Tips for Setting Up Multiple Streams of Passive Income Using Affiliate Marketing and More

Contents

Part 1: Blogging For Beginners

Proven Strategies for Marketing Your Blog in 2020 and Making a Profit with Your Writing by Creating Multiple Streams of Passive Income

Introduction

You have probably heard much conflicting information about blogging in 2020. Some people swear it is the exploding business platform of the future, while others claim it is dead or dying. How do you know which is true? Take a moment to examine your perception and participation with blogs. Do you find them valuable? Interesting? Engaging? Relevant? Do you find tips and techniques through various forms of information shared online by real users, not companies? If you answered yes to any or all of these, then you are living proof that blogging is still alive and very relevant for 2020. And you are the perfect person to begin making a full-time income using your voice online.

You can sift through a lot of information online about how to get started blogging, but it can be hard when some of the information is designed for the hobby blog and blogger. These are people just putting out ideas and content because it is their personal outlet, not to make money. You are here because you want to do that to some extent, but you want to get paid for it. The purpose of this book is to help you get started with your blog and making money in a real and applicable way.

Get excited to learn about the basics of blogging and money making, how to get it all started, and how to share it with others. You will also learn about various ideas to help you generate income through your blog as well as how to move blogging from a part-time side-hustle to generating a full-time income.

Chapter 1: Blogging for Profit – The Basics You Need to Know

Can You Really Make Money Blogging?

So, you know what a blog is, you know that people make money doing it, and you want to get in on the action. But do you really know how it makes you money? And is it really feasible to think that a blog can make a "day-job" be sustainable income? There are a few ways a blog makes money, and it depends on what you want to talk about and how you want to approach your blogging career. The purpose of this section is just to get you thinking about some different topics, which will be explored in more detail later in the book. In addition, you will have the opportunity to take a short "quiz" to help you figure out just what "kind" of blogger you are so you can start customizing your blog and your monetization accordingly.

Below is a list of different ways many bloggers make money through their sites. Again, you will learn more about what these really are, how they work, and if they make sense for your style of blog. However, right now, you can see the many different methods used that you can pick and choose from later.

1. Cost Per Click, or CPC
2. Pay Per Click, or PPC
3. Cost Per 1,000 Impressions, or CPM
4. Private advertising space
5. Affiliate links
6. Sell online services or products such as:
    a. E-books
    b. Online workshops and courses
    c. Music, videos, and images that can be re-used in other's content
7. Content marketing
8. Memberships

Sometimes, simply creating valuable content and sharing advice is important enough that people will begin to see you as a resource and expert. You will become the name and business they associate with your industry. When they need something from your sector, you are the first stop on their purchasing journey. This can take a long time to establish. However, when you can generate followers in this manner and develop your reputation in this way, it is one of the most successful ways of building an income stream from blogging. Of course, this is best done for the Corporate or Entrepreneur blogger.

This leads into the different bloggers you may interact with and can help determine where you fall in the mix of all of this. Below is a quick introduction to some of the various types of bloggers online today:

1. *The Entrepreneur*: This person is blogging for their business. Sometimes, the blog is their business, while other times, they have another business that they are promoting through the use of their blog.

2. *The Corporate*: While blogging, Corporate is building content and a reputation for their company. Blogging may not be their full-time job, but they spend a considerable amount of their time focused on it.

3. *The Full-Time Pro*: You will see this pop up from time to time on a job board or company website, "blogger for hire." This position is brought into a company for the sole purpose of writing, monitoring, and managing their online presence, specifically their blog. This role creates content for the site, and also finds guest contributors or contributes to other blogs in an effort to raise awareness for this company's site.

4. *The Part-Time Pro*: Unlike the Entrepreneur or Full Time Pro, this person has a completely separate job. This job may influence the blog, but it is not about the business or company necessarily. This is the supplemental income-type of a blog.

5. *The Hobbyist*: Sometimes, a blog is just meant to be fun. Sure, it can turn into something more lucrative someday, but sometimes, it is enjoyable just to put things out there to share with others. Contributions are usually just a few times a week, and there is no real income generated through this content.

You may easily determine right now how you fall into these categories, or you may be swaying from one area to the next. For example, if you own a business, you could be deciding if you want to blog as part of that business, do something separate as a Part-Time Pro, or even just create a blog as a Hobbyist. If you do not own a business, you have the choice of being a Part-Time Pro, Hobbyist, or even an Entrepreneur. You can also approach your current company to ask about becoming a corporate content marketing professional as part of your role. To help you determine what the best fit is for you, take the quiz below and find out!

1. When you think about writing a blog post that is new and engaging, you feel:
   a. YAY! This is going to be awesome!
   b. I'm not sure I have the time to start and finish that project...
   c. Okay, but how is it going to make me money?

d. AH! I'm staring at a blank page and can think of nothing to write!

2. What kind of content do you like to engage with, make, or think you want to make?

    a. Your favorite things with reviews or styled images.

    b. Tips for travel such as booking suggestions and itineraries for favorite places.

    c. How-tos with detailed instructions.

    d. A piece that highlights my personality and full of personal content.

3. What ways will you publish your content or do you think will make sense for you when blogging?

    a. Through personal social sites like Facebook and Instagram to the general public.

    b. Online groups and forums.

    c. Using a service like Co-Schedule, Hootsuite, or Buffer to schedule your posts.

    d. Only to my friends and family through Facebook or a single social site.

4. What statement below feels like it fits best with your goals or ideas about blogging?

    a. My blog needs to reflect my passions. I realize that not all my ideas and passions are "money makers", but I want to find something that I love that can also generate an income stream.

    b. While money is the primary object of my blog, I want to use the influence of the blog and the money it generates to not only fuel my dreams but help others as well.

    c. I want to make money. It does not matter what the content is about; all I care about is making money. That is my inspiration.

    d. The desire to make a difference in the world through my purpose and passion are the only reasons for me putting myself out there like this.

5. The last time you went shopping you bought:

    a. New high heels that were on display in the window of the fancy store you like.

    b. A backpack, travel bag, or suitcase.

    c. An online training, workshop or class.

    d. A fresh notebook because all of your other notebooks are filled with stories, musings, and ideas. Or you bought it because you love the idea of selecting an opportunity for words of wisdom.

6. Fill in the last of this sentence, "Right now, I would rather be…"

    a. Shopping for the latest styles and accessories.

    b. Traveling to somewhere new and/or exciting.

    c. Making money!

    d. Writing! Anything and everything, just getting it out on "paper".

7. Imagine you have posted a new blog post and a few people have started leaving comments. What do you think people will say about your writing?

    a. "Great find! It is so perfect. I need to buy this for my wardrobe/house/etc."

    b. "What an experience! Thanks for sharing."

    c. "Thank you! This was super helpful."

    d. "This is the funniest thing ever!"

8. Choose the statement that best fits your personality:

    a. You never know who is watching or when an opportunity arrives, so always dress your best. After all, your world is your stage!

    b. You are not afraid of seeking adventure. In fact, you crave finding something new to explore near and far.

    c. What you know you have to teach. When you learn something new, you want to share it with others to help them with their learning.

d. I love so many areas of life; it is hard to pick just one! When I learn something new, I want to go all in and find out more and more. I am passionate about many areas of life.

If you answered mainly "a": You are setting trends. Maybe it is not about fashion; maybe it is about the home or another trend, but you are spotting it and rocking it, and others tune in to learn from you. It is a form of "hobbyist" but can turn into a great entrepreneurial or part-time professional path.

If you answered mainly "b": You are moving and grooving, and people want to see it. You share your experiences for a number of reasons, but the primary one is that you are passionate about it. You could be doing this as part of a position, meaning you are Full-Time blogger or Part Time Professional, but you can also pursue this path as a Hobbyist.

If you answered mainly "c": You are a business blogger. You are most likely doing this as a full-time job or part of a job.

If you answered mainly "d": You are a lifestyle, hobby blogger. You may turn it into something financially supportive or maybe something part time, but most of the time, you are turning to this outlet for your passions rather than a purse.

When you are a Travel Blogger…

You are a thrill seeker and want to reflect your adventures. You live a life full of passion and excitement, or at least you want to. The idea of your blog as a way to live this lifestyle all the time or more often is attractive to you. You are looking to use it to fund your adventures or at least encourage you to do it more often.

It is likely that you search for and embrace new opportunities. You like to be flexible and free to do what you want. You also do not do well with a project that does not inspire you, no matter how much money you can make from it. This is where you could pursue your blog as a Hobbyist, rather than for income. On the other hand, you could use the monetization of your blog to fund your travels and life. To help you make money with this type of blog, consider finding brands and businesses that support your travel interests. These brands can provide affiliate links, paid advertisements, or PPC.

When you are a Trendsetting Blogger...

You are looking for the newest "hot" topic or item. You are the person that people go to in order to learn about the latest and greatest. You always are watching what people are doing and talking about and bringing it into your life in some way. This can be fashion related, or it can be about technology, design, food, or more. You are also a host of tips, tricks, and techniques on the latest new thing.

Sometimes, this pursuit can seem uncertain because you are pioneering the way and are not sure if anyone is going to follow along. This is normal for this position; trust in your ability to see what is coming and bring new light to an area that needs it. Some things will fail, but most likely you are on top of topics, ensuring your success on the upward trajectory. This is a business and profit-making blog. Sometimes, this is connected to another business, making you a Full Time or Part Time Professional. Occasionally, you will see this type of role also categorized as a corporate blogger. Consider adding affiliate links to your site for best monetization.

When you are a Lifestyle, Blogger...

You are a being with many interests. You can not really surprise those that you are close to because they know just how dynamic you really are. Sometimes, it is hard to stick to one topic for a long time because you have so many interests—it is hard to pick. This means your blog could cover a host of topics like fashion, home, beauty, cooking, travel, etc. The topics you share are often instructional and inspirational. People like to read what you have to say because it is so passionate and diverse. Most of the time, the topic in these blogs is shared amongst friends and neighbors because of the connection to their lives. This is an in-demand field because of its power to influence. This means you can find yourself successful as a Part-

Time Pro, a Full-Time Professional, or Entrepreneur. In addition, you can pursue this as pure passion being a Hobbyist. It can be a challenge if you are a Corporate blogger because this is a heavy passion project. It can also be a challenge as a Full-Time Professional if your business is not multi-faceted and you are not passionate about what they are offering to the community.

Monetization can occur in almost any way you decide, and that does not interfere with your passion presentation. Make sure your personality is not overshadowed by the advertising and affiliate links for the best success.

When you are a Business Blogger…

You are knowledgeable and experienced. You know your industry, whatever that is, and are willing to share some of what you have learned along the way. Other times, you have a new idea that you want to introduce to the industry and need a platform to present the idea and vet it for fresh perspectives. This is also a very passionate outlet for sharing messages, but often, the driver of money and profit is what motivates you more than the desire to share information. Not always, but often. Do not let this drive for income overtake your unique perspective, offerings, and voice. That is what sets your business apart from the competition, so let it shine in your blog too. Also, do not get so caught up in monetization that you miss the content. You will not make money if your blog posts are not engaging. Keep your audience and customers in mind before the money, and you will bring in both well.

Blogging in 2020: Why Do It Now

Ten years ago, blogging was a completely different "animal" than it is today. Before, it was just a simple platform for sharing ramblings or advice. Now, they are stylish, well-organized, and responsive. Algorithms have been updated to favor the blog topics. Of course, with these advances, more people are flocking to the medium, making for more competition than before. However, while there is competition, you have an amazing opportunity. Now, more than ever, people are looking for honest and real reviews, experiences, and tutorials. People are looking for real-life information more than advertisements online or websites offering information provided by the business. For example, one of the most popular features on Amazon is the filter for average reviews. People make their purchasing decision based on the reviews of other shoppers more than the description of the product and even the price.

Some advice floating around is that no one wants to read long posts, so keep your content short and sweet, or people are only watching videos, so do not waste your time writing down something you can show them. The truth is that people are interacting with the written word through blog formats more than ever, in addition to short tutorials or commentary and videos. Blogging is a viable method for making money, building a business, and following your passions. Now, also more than ever, you can find an outlet for your creativity and passion that others are also searching for. In the age where the Internet and access are with us at all times, you can offer information in a valuable and personal way. People are searching for a personal connection, and your voice may be just the thing they are looking for. In addition, incorporating various income streams help safeguard you against economic impacts like the Recession. There are just so many benefits to blogging that it makes sense to get started now. It is not too late to create an outlet and make some money doing it.

Why You Need a Niche

Once you decide that you are going to start blogging and choose what type of blogger you are going to start out as, then you need to know what you are going to write about. Yes, like a Hobbyist or Lifestyle blogger, you can cover a myriad of topics, but most of the time, you want to boil it down to something predictable and comprehensive. People are looking online to find information about something; usually, a question or problem they have and they need an answer. If they find your blog, you better work on presenting that information to them in a helpful and clear way. Rambling on will not solve their problems! Choosing a niche means you narrow down your audience and tailor your content to their needs. For example, you provide fashion advice to the working mom or travel tips to the millennial. Not only do you find a small group to talk to, but you give them content they value, so they keep coming back.

Finding this niche is not always an easy task. It could be like staring at a blank page urging words to come, or you could feel like you are swimming in a sea of ideas and choosing one is like grasping a single water drop. The simple place to start is to settle on what you are passionate about. Passion is what breathes behind all successful blogs. If you love what you are writing and sharing, your readers will feel it. This keeps them connected and wanting to be a part of it. In addition, your passion motivates you to put more time into the project and can sustain your efforts for a longer period. It can take months for your blog to start making real money and focusing on a passion can help you get there. Passion also has very few limits. You can probably find a million things to talk about when it comes to something you love.

If the idea of finding or uncovering a "passion" seems daunting, begin by listing out things that you do such as hobbies or activities you participate in during your free time. Is there something that your friends and family joke about like "opening a can of worms" when someone brings the topic up around you? Was there something in school or in your earlier years that you loved learning about or doing? This could include something that you read or took a class on and still want more. Another way to look at is like you get to choose one thing you can do for the rest of your life. What would that one thing be? You may think everyone will say the same thing, but in reality, your dreams and passions may be just different enough from what is out there and still resonate with a whole group of people.

Below is a list of questions you should answer to help pinpoint a potential niche for your blog. You can use this to guide you or follow your own instincts:

1. List out all your hobbies or activities or that you wish were your hobbies.

2. List out things you enjoy doing or that you think you would enjoy doing.

3. Think about how you spend your free time or would want to spend your free time and write down what you do.

4. If you were asked for advice on a specific topic, what is one thing you could speak about with confidence and knowledge for awhile?

5. When you were a little child, what activities did you love? What was the most fun thing you remember as a child?

6. Do you take classes or workshops on something? Do you want to learn more about a specific topic? What area have you done the most training in?

It is okay if you choose something and are still unsure of the niche. Get into your blog and start putting content out there. If your niche begins to transform and move with your passion and audience, that is great! If you settle into the niche and begin to dominate the market, that is great too! No, you do not want to bounce around from topic to topic without a plan, but you are also not tied down to one niche for the rest of your life. You can let it naturally evolve with the people you are engaging and your interests.

To dominate your niche, you need to know your niche. You need to offer content that engages your niche. When you get in this sweet spot, you are now ready to bring up the interaction a notch. Maybe you do something different that has not been done before, or cover a hot topic in a new way, or even expand on something that was a popular discussion a month or so ago. Find holes in your competition's information and add a fresh spin to old topics. In addition to finding a great fit for an audience, you will also find a great fit for advertisers and businesses. As you start to partner with businesses on your site for promotion and monetization, you can make sure that the brands you bring on really do fit with your audience and they can easily see this fit through the content you are posting and the comments of the people engaging with you.

Some people choose to go through a network rather than a niche and independent blog. That is an okay method for promoting work and content; however, if you want to make a profit targeting a select group of people, having an independent blog with a clear niche is a much more lucrative approach. Niches and networks do not mix well together. A network can provide income faster than a stand-alone blog; however, your blog offers freedom of frequency, and you can pocket all the profits.

Passive Income Explained

Blogging is not a passive activity. It takes time, dedication, and effort. Sometimes, people get confused with blogging activity and the idea of "making money while you sleep". Your blog can bring money to you while you are sleeping because of the effort you put into it while you were awake. It is not something you can just set and then forget about and start making a ton of cash. This is very important to remember. With that knowledge, you can move forward and create an amazing blog that keeps bringing you new sources of income. There are a few things you can do now that can continue to bring you income long term. Below is a list of different income generators that have a great "shelf life:"

> • *Personal templates and checklists.* What are you blogging about? Are you sharing information about your financial knowledge? What tool can you develop that would be valuable to your readers to use? Think of an Excel budgeting tool or tracker. Are you writing about travel? Create a guidebook with tips for visiting different places you have been or a list for how to effectively pack a suitcase for international travel. Once you create this, make it easy for your readers to find on your blog and promote it. The more the word gets out about how awesome it is, the more people are going to buy it and continue to buy it for a long time.

• *Give dropshipping a try.* You can sell physical items on your blog that correlate with your niche but never actually hold any inventory personally. This is called dropshipping. There are various companies out there that will produce the inventory and hold it until you tell them what to ship and to where. There are many suppliers and methods you can choose from to add this feature to your site. It would be wise to set up a system for monitoring your sales and communicating with your supplier, but the front end work can be worth all the passive income on the backend.

• *Share your knowledge in more detail.* If you are an "expert" or very knowledgeable about a certain topic, the chances are that you could write for days on it and share a ton of information. Maybe you have shared a bunch of it already but keep getting requests for more on different areas. And in the digital world, you do not need to worry about selling a physical book. Create a digital e-book and sell it on your site. Set it at a reasonable price and promote it to your readers and through an auto-responder email function. Once you write the book, it is an "evergreen" product you can sell passively for years and years.

• *Promote what you use for profit.* If you are writing about a topic on your blog, it is probably because you are passionate about that area in your personal or professional life. This also means that you are probably using products related to this area in some way. You will learn more about affiliate links, but the basics are this: when you talk about a product on your blog, add a link for the reader to purchase it. When the reader buys that product from your link, you get a portion of the sales. If you are already using the products and services, it is a great "win-win".

• *Create a custom course.* This is especially helpful if you are sharing knowledge and tips already on a topic. Professional and Corporate bloggers can rock this income opportunity, develop a course on a teaching platform and sell it to your readers. You can offer an in-person course, but that can be a challenge with people not signing up in time or not enough signed up to dedicate the time to it. Instead, consider offering a pre-recorded class that readers can download or receive over a series of weeks to learn the skills. The added benefit of this passive income option is that you can charge a good amount for what you have to offer.

• *Challenge your readers to change their life.* When you see that your readers are looking to make meaningful changes in their lives, you can help them push outside of their comfort zones. Creating a fun and engaging challenge that can help your readers make real, positive changes in their lives can be valuable. This can be a pre-recorded presentation, or it could be an email series with information and accountability built into it. Once you set it up, promote it, and watch it keep making you money for years to come.

Earning money while you share your passion and knowledge with your readers is a goal, not a dream. You can make it happen with a plan and action. There are many things you can do to make that money, even more than the quick list above, but never forget that the act of blogging is not a passive process. You must still generate content that engages and reaches your readers. This takes time and effort. The things you do in support of this can bring in passive income in addition to the other income streams you develop for your site. In addition, not all forms of passive income make sense for what you have to offer to your niche audience. Make sure to choose something that is worthwhile to your readers and that you can realistically offer them. For example, a training course may be a challenge for a travel blogger but could be great for a tech blogger that can share how to get the most out of smart home features. A challenge may not fit with your readers who come to you for funny quips and fashion reviews, but it works great for a beauty blogger encouraging their readers to embrace a safer or more affordable approach to their appearance.

Take the time to think about what you think you could add to your readers and their experience with your blog in a meaningful and realistic way. Maybe you already have thought up some options to add to your site, or you are still rolling the ideas around to see what will stick with the words you are offering to readers. Whatever you decide to do, for the best passive income strategies, choose to spend your time on something that will continue to make your income well after you put it out for sale.

Success Stories: Bloggers Who Earn $10,000+ a Month

There are "real" bloggers out there making "real" money with what they have grown and created. The idea of making money through writing about your passion online is not unrealistic or out of reach. First, look at some bloggers and blogs that are making a great amount of money:

1. Huffington Post: $2,330,000/month
2. Mashable: $560,000/month
3. Perez Hilton: $450,000/month
4. Techcrunch: $400,000/month
5. Smashing Magazine: $190,000/month
6. Timothy Sykes: $150,000/month
7. Gothamist: $110,000/month
8. Tuts Plus: $110,000/month
9. Car Advice: $70,000/month
10. Venture Beat: $62,000/month

These blogs have invested time and resources into building them into the success they are today. This is possible, but you have to do the leg work as they have in order to see their level of success. On the other hand, there are "everyday bloggers" that are also making a good amount of money each month that you can learn from. The following list of people are some bloggers who make $10,000/month or more:

- Jorden Makelle
- Jeff Rose
- Natalie Bacon
- Greg Kononenko
- Allison Lindstrom
- Morgan Timm
- Lena Gott
- Ramit Sethi
- Matthew Woodward
- Pat Flynn
- Neil Patel

These people have also invested time and effort into building their blogging platform and reaching readers but in a different way. You can do this too! Below are some tips that these people have shared to help you find your success in getting started with blogging to produce an income:

1. Find the "fruit" that is hanging in a particular topic or niche. Search with popular and trending keywords and look for things that are missing. That is your opportunity.

2. Be smart about your content. Cut long posts into smaller chunks and repurpose topics that could benefit from video or infographics, for example.

3. Be clear about what the reader is going to experience throughout your post. Use headings, subheadings, snippets, call out's, images, etc., to help guide and inform your reader through your content.

4. Pay attention to what counts. The content that converts is the content you should focus on. This allows you to drive more traffic to those converting pages but also gives you a format for developing converting content again in the future.

5. Start small and grow big. This includes your reach but also your ideas. If you think something will resonate, test it out for free to gauge the response. If it is hitting the target on the

small set, go all out with a paid advertisement to promote it to more people. This approach helps you determine what is best to spend your money on and what is best to be left as a pleasant surprise for readers but did not cost you in advertising. Your posts should also be "small" in the sense that it should cover one topic and offer one solution. Be specific with the solution in one post. If there is more than one solution, turn it into a series and grow the information in multiple posts rather than one long, intense one.

6. Grow loyalty, not fans. Having a million fans on your pages is great, but only if a good amount of them are doing more than just skimming your headlines now and then. Instead, focus your attention on growing a loyal group of converting readers.

7. When you begin, offer great value for free. For example, if you are working on a course that you want to sell through your blog, offer tips on the subject for free through your blog or free downloads with great content that leads well into the topic of your course. This way, you establish a reputation as knowledgeable and helpful, and readers will know the value of your work and why you are charging for it in the future. This is also a great method for having a high price for a product or service and getting real customers to engage with it.

8. Keep a calendar and block off time to dedicate to this. You want to make sure you are consistent and in touch. Give yourself time every week to review what is relevant to your audience, come up with ideas for content, and enough time to create and edit it. You can always prepare ahead of time and set content to auto-publish on a specific day and time, but you always want to keep a pulse on your readers. This means doing your research and taking the time to make this something valuable.

Chapter 2: Starting Your Blog

Getting Started: Platforms, Hosting, Domains

Welcome to the world of setting up a blog site or platform. This can become a bit confusing because there are a variety of different options out there for you to consider, and all of the hosting sites you look at will say they are the best. This is not wrong; they are all great in one way or another, but there are some very important things you need to know at the start to help you choose the best domain, host, or platform for your money-making blog.

Remember that your blog is a site focused on writing content that is valuable to your audience and niche. You can include things like audio, images, and video, but the focus is on the written word. It is great to have a clear and active place for people to comment on your content. This way you have a connection to your readers directly and can use this interaction to form your future content. It is also how readers can learn to trust your position as a leader in your area. This does not mean you need to be a true "expert" or "leader" in an industry, but rather you are leading the conversation on the topic you presented in a personal and knowledgeable way. This is where passion plays a big part. However, since you already know this, now you need to know how to set it up and in a way that is best for making money.

There are six basic steps for starting your blog:

1. Choose a name
2. Choose a hosting site and register your blog name
3. Select a template for your blog and set it up
4. Create your content and post it to your site
5. Make sure to insert one or more ways for your content to generate money for you
6. Promote your content across the Internet

As you begin choosing the name for your blog, you will be looking at domain names as well. This is because someone may have already scooped up your great idea for a blog or website name! No sense in getting all ready to publish a new blog that does not have a domain name that matches it. This does not mean your domain name needs to match your blog name exactly, but it should be clear and obvious in the connection. If you run into a situation where your domain name is taken, try the name with a different extension. For example, if you wanted **www.blogblog.com,** but it is taken, check to see if **www.blogblog.net** or **www.blogblog.org** is available. The .com extension is the most popular, but it may not be the best for your site or content. If that still does not do it, try adding in a short word to the domain name, like **www.MyBlogBlog.com** or **www.ABlogBlog.com**. Another idea is to add dashes between the words. Spaces are not allowed in a domain name, but a well-placed dash can work wonders. To continue with the example, it would look something like **www.My-Blog-Blog.com**.

Once you determine your domain name, you are ready to get your content online. Thankfully, with all the hosting sites and platforms to choose from out there, you can choose something that you like, and that fits your budget. A host or hosting site is a place that puts all the things you will most likely need into one neat package so your users can experience a professional and functional interaction. It is necessary to have a host for your blog. You can always build yours from the ground up, or you can work with a company that has it pretty easy and simple to get going. Software or hosts or platforms for blogs are all a little different, but some of the most popular are:

1. Wordpress
2. Wix
3. Blogger
4. Tumblr
5. Medium
6. Squarespace
7. Joomla
8. Ghost
9. Weebly

Before you start slogging through all the in's and out's of each hosting site or platform, you want to make sure you choose a platform that is easy to use and has the growth you plan for your blog. This requires an opportunity for growth if you want it. If you choose a platform now because it is free or inexpensive, it could be a big pain later when you want to change. And, obviously, you want to make sure your choice is set up to allow you to make money easily!

Below is a quick Pro/Con list of the platforms mentioned above:

WordPress

Pro: Control over all parts of your site. Popular. Allows for growth. Offers extra features like forums and paid memberships. Many free templates and plug-ins. SEO friendly.

Con: Backup and security are on you. It does require some training and a learning curve.

Cost: Free up to $23/year.

Wix

Pro: Plenty of options for customization. No coding necessary. Easy to use. Set up is quick.

Con: Limited free functions. Changing a template or background is nearly impossible to do. E-commerce is limited.

Cost: Free to $25/month.

Blogger

Pro: Free. Easy to manage and utilize without a tech background. Supported by Google. Reliable and secure.

Con: Limited and basic. Cannot add new features as your blog grows. Few templates to choose from. Updates are infrequent. Google has control over your blog and can suspend or cancel it without notice.

Cost: Free.

Tumblr

Pro: Free with Tumblr subdomain. Ease of use and set up. Social media is well integrated. Offers a micro-blog option which can be beneficial for short posts like GIF's, images, and audio.

Con: Features are limited that could dampen your growth. No additional features for their various templates. Importing or backing up your blog is a challenge.

Cost: Free.

Medium

Pro: No coding or setup skills required. Easy to start. Can connect to an existing online community with like-minded interests. The focus is on writing a great blog, not on design.

Con: Very limited features. Your audience is on Medium, so if you leave or move your blog to a new host, you lose your audience. Not a customized domain name. Money making opportunities are limited.

Cost: Free.

Squarespace

Pro: Simple, professional templates. Offers other domain names with e-commerce opportunity.

Con: Limited features. Integration is limited.

Cost: Varies up to $40/month.

Joomla

Pro: Powerful to build just about any type of site. Hundreds of templates. Extensions available.

Con: Small community. Limited support. Security, updates, and backup is your responsibility.

Cost: Free to $23/month.

Ghost

Pro: Blog and writing focus. Intuitive interface. JavaScript for speed. Setup is not required.

Con: Customization with apps is a challenge. Limited options including themes. Can be complicated to install on your own.

Cost: Free to $29/month.

Weebly

Pro: Drag-and-drop usability. Quick setup. Try out services before paying for them.

Con: Features cannot be added to templates. Third-party integration is limited. Changing your blog to another site is challenging.

Cost: Free to $38/month.

Money-Making Niches: Which One's yours?

You are looking to make money, but you also want to focus on something you are interested in. In fact, the best way to choose a niche is to pick topics you enjoy and feel fulfilled by, but also create content that reaches your audience. Your targeted readers should be looking for and demanding your content. Once you find this intersection, it is time to look at how you can make a profit through monetization. If you can figure out ways to profit from that combination, you have found a great niche. Now, the level of monetization, demand, or fulfillment is up to you. You could choose something that you are completely fulfilled by but do not make a lot or any money from; this is the Hobbyist blogger. On the other hand, you could choose a niche that you know will make you a lot of money but is one you are not as passionate about; this is a Full-Time Professional or Corporate blogger. Neither of these "extremes" is bad, but it is just what is best for you.

Below is a breakdown out of different niche approaches depending on your preference: *passion, monetization, or demand.*

Passion

The old saying, "Follow your passions and success will follow," is not as easy as it sounds. In reality, your passion needs to be fueled and developed by hard work and effort. Instead of approaching this arena from a personal perspective, as in "What can this niche do for me?" consider it from the view of, "What can I offer to others?" Approaching your passion in this way is what ensures that it makes you money and brings success. Share what you know in a way that helps others with their problems, so you do not just "toot your horn".

Monetization

To determine the profitability of your niche, look to the competition. If there are many others in your niche, you have an opportunity. If you know these blogs are making money, and good money, you are in the right spot. Competition is good in blogging because everyone has a personality and perspective. Yours can be valuable too.

Demand

When you are approaching passion in a serving manner instead of the selfish way, you are creating content of value. This leads very well to demand. People want value, and that is what you have got. The more people you can help, the better the demand for your voice. As you figure out the problems of others and how your interests and experiences help them, the more successful you will become. This success is what leads to more profit opportunity.

Common Niche Themes

- Business Blogs: Marketing blogs are especially popular and have a lot of competition. Remember: this is not bad! People want help, and you can help them! Now, just because you have a voice, though, you are still going to be talking alongside some of the brightest professionals in your field. This could mean that you focus your content to a field that does not have "great" marketing skills already. The great thing about this niche is that you can offer services and products for top-dollar and sharpen your skills. On the other hand, competition is high level.

- Hobby Blogs: This is a big niche, especially on the social platform Pinterest. You can quickly and easily build a successful blog in this area when you leverage the connection to Pinterest. There is great potential for SEO, and you can easily sell products on sites like Etsy and Shopify. Unfortunately, the price of products is often lower than other niches.

- Culinary Blogs: Advertising is the biggest revenue stream for culinary blogs. Unfortunately, this means that many people need to get to your site first before it starts making money. This visitation can happen quickly if you have a strong Pinterest strategy. Social media and SEO are ripe with demand for topics on culinary trends. In addition, there is much opportunity for sponsored posts from various brands. If you can react fast on a trend, you can make a big impact. On the other hand, coming up with a great recipe with quality photos and testing can take a lot of time. Also, most people are coming to these sites for free recipes. Selling products is hard when you are giving away their demand for free.

- Fashion or Apparel Blogs: Talk about visuals! This is great for social sites like Pinterest, YouTube, and Instagram. You can monetize this easily with affiliate marketing, content that is sponsored, and through advertisements. Monetization is easy to accomplish with this type of niche. In addition, the competition is not as high level. However, the problem with a fashion blog is that it is all about you and your visual life. Also, you are not typically able to sell high-priced items.

• Investing and Finance Blogs: Money does not need to just center on people interested in the finance industry. People of all walks of life and careers are looking for ways to save money, make money, cut back on spending, increase investing, etc. It is a "hot" topic on Pinterest. Use this traffic-generator to increase visitors to your site, and then capitalize with a great SEO strategy. You can focus on just about any area of investing or finance, but the area you can make the most money and charge the most is focusing on how people can make money. The best ways to capture this is by building a big readership and then introducing how to make money. There is no shortage of people looking for this information, so you should have no problems building your readership. Just remember: people, are looking for this type of information rather seasonally, typically between November and February. Also, large businesses are pursuing this niche as well so you will be competing with companies with a lot of money invested in this arena.

• Fitness-focused Blogs: For new bloggers in this field, get on to Pinterest immediately and start driving traffic to your blog. You will quickly gain a large readership. People are looking for information and solutions to their health and wellness. The best way to make money, and the most common, is with affiliate links. If you have it already or plan on it, you can develop your products to solve your reader's problems, and this is a great money-making approach. The great thing about this niche is the variety of ways you can generate revenue. The challenge, however, is that there is much competition in this niche and it is also a seasonal group, typically peaking in January.

• Lifestyle Blogs: This tilting can be misleading. This type of approach is really a multiple niche approach. The attraction is that you do not have to narrow down what interest you are going to focus on; however, you do still need to select topics that will drive readership. Pinterest is the popular social site for these blogs, and the users want visually engaging "hot" topics. In addition, the successful blogs in this arena are targeting a demographic. They are selecting topics to talk about that the majority of people in that "group" are going to be interested in. For example, mom lifestyle bloggers cover topics like caring for a newborn, the best way to travel with toddlers, how to feed a family on a budget, etc. This type of approach allows you to switch up your content based on what is trending and you will probably never get bored or burnt out because you can always change what you are working on. This format also opens the door for many diverse revenue opportunities. But on the other hand, spreading out your content across topics means you spread out your impact on SEO. In addition, targeting just a demographic and not a specific area means that your readers are coming for a variety of answers to their questions. It can be a challenge to develop a strong content marketing strategy when your readership is so diverse.

• Travel Blogs: Travel blogs are not just about sharing awesome pictures of places you have traveled, although it can be a part of it. Instead, a successful travel blog highlights interesting places that a certain group of people would be interested in visiting. The content is meant to inspire this audience to do something adventurous, too, even if it is not to travel to the place you blogged about. Drive traffic to this type of blog through various social sites, including Pinterest. You also do not need to just talk about places to visit on this platform; instead, think about offering advice about how to make money while traveling or different hacks for the best travel experiences. You can also make money from readers signing up for credit cards that target travelers. Keep in mind, however, that most successful blogs do include your personal travels. This means you must be willing to travel a lot for a long time. This can mean spending a lot of money up front before your blog becomes successful. In addition, the money readers are spending is on their travel plans. This limits your opportunity to generate money directly from them.

Know Your Enemy (aka Competitors)

Just about every great coach in the history of coaching knows that to aide your success in the game, you need to know whom you are competing against. This allows them to develop specific strategies to help them win when they get on the field. There are a million excuses not to do this; including not wanting to "stalk" someone or the idea is so great that there is no need to see what others are doing, or there is no time to look at the competition. The reality is that sooner or later, all money makers need to lift their head up from their work and look at what is happening around them. The most successful do this early before making many unnecessary mistakes. Knowing your competition, or your "enemy", gives you a great picture of where you sit in relation to the rest of the market and also offers the opportunity to develop new and valuable ideas for your readers.

It can be overwhelming to start getting to know your competition. The best place to start is through Google. If you have a niche or topic or product you want to blog about, look it up on Google. Try different keywords associated with it. If you know the question or problem you want to solve, type it into Google and see what answers are offered already. Also, look on the App store and other marketplaces to see if there is some sort of product or service that solves the problem already. Make sure you look at the two different kinds of competition while doing your research. The two different kinds of competition are direct competition, or those offering solutions to the same problem, and the indirect competition. Indirect competition is those who offer something very different but to your target audience or they offer the same type of solution but to a different group of people. The value of knowing your indirect competition is how a person will find a solution to their problem, even if the messaging is not made for them. When you find this out, you can now find a way to offer a unique solution meant just for them.

To keep track of your information, create a competition spreadsheet. Compile all the information about the competition including the branding, target audience, and products offered. If possible, try their products. Engage with their content. If you are struggling with or cannot experience all the competition has to offer, see if you can read reviews and customer experiences. To help you format your spreadsheet, consider the following information:

1. *Identification*. Make a column for the name of the competition, the URL, and if you consider them to be direct or indirect.

2. *Summary*: write one or two sentences about what you discovered in your research. This can include the values, target audience, product offerings, personality, etc. Anything that stands out to you about the competition can be mentioned here.

3. *Advantages*: What is this competitor doing that is awesome? What things are they offering that you would also want to offer?

4. *Challenges*: Find areas that your competition is missing or failing at, and read reviews and forums to find areas of opportunity.

5. *Money makers*: How is your competition making money that you can easily see?

6. *Numerical data*: List how many people follow the competition on various social sites, their website, etc. How many downloads does their app or other products get per month? The information does not have to be super accurate, but it should be reflective of your impression. It may make

sense to offer a separate sub-column for each data set. You can also include the average or range of prices if the competition is offering products or services for sale.

Once you compile all this data, look at it from a big-picture view. Do not look at each competitor right now, but instead, see if you can identify a theme or major hole. You can also notice if something is working across the competition. For example, are all the competitors offering a similar product or solution? Are they all reaching the audience through a strong presence on a social media site? You want to look for what the group is doing that is working and what is still being "left on the table". Once you get the "big picture", you can move to look at each one individually and begin developing a strategy.

Now that you have all the information, you can figure out what you are going to do on your blog so that it is different from your competition as well as knowing the problems to solve. In this strategy, you are also going to begin to outline the way you plan on bringing this to your audience. This is one of the most important steps in blogging for profit. This is essential for you to succeed and thrive. It is how you offer value to your customer time and time again. Do *not* skip this step.

Integrating Social Media

It should be no surprise that social media is the best method for getting people to learn about your blog and content, but how do you effectively share this information across various sites? And which sites should you focus on for the best results? And how often should you post to them? There is so much information surrounding this topic alone, but the following information is designed to introduce you to the wide world of social media and what you can do to get your blog out there. First, learn about cross promoting. It can be as simple as just sharing the same message on a variety of platforms, but remember that you do need to make some adjustments for the audience. You cannot just copy and paste.

One of the reasons you need to change up your post from one site to the other is because there is a different audience on each site. They go to that social platform for different reasons. For example, a person may go to Pinterest to see images and find links connected to a topic they are interested in, typically a DIY topic. They do not go on LinkedIn to find a tutorial on how to bake the best banana bread or how to refinish a mid-century modern chair. They visit LinkedIn to learn more information about their career in human resources and find new candidates for an open position. Also, each platform has its post preferences and restrictions. For example, you may have a great short article you share in a post on Facebook, but Twitter makes you cut it down to no more than 140 characters. Below is a breakdown of some information you should know for a few popular social media sites you will want to consider using for blog post promotion:

1. Facebook
- "Share" and "Like" content
- Easy place for promoting blog posts in a group, page, or personal profile
- Posts can be up to 10,000 characters; however, the first 480 characters are the only ones visible in the feed
- Long posts are not as engaging. Try to keep it to 50 characters or less
- Add images for the best response
- When you upload an image with a post, it is stored in a photo album. This allows followers to be able to view your images separately from your posts
- Hashtags do not work extremely well on Facebook, but they do help it become more searchable
- Ask readers to comment and share on your posts with personal messages
- Most frequented times for Facebook are 1-4PM and 6-10PM and all day Saturday and Sunday
- Try to post once a day

- Share posts on your profile, page, and groups, but vary when you share it and change the message in the text for each share

2. Twitter

- "Tweets" and "Re-Tweets"
- Limited text message no more than 140 characters
- Images are now allowed and do help increase re-tweets
- Adding links to tweets is also good for increasing re-tweets
- Always have more than four hashtags in a post to increase the searchability of the content and increase reactions to the content
- To increase results, add a call-to-action
- Most frequented times for Twitter are 8-10AM, 11AM-1PM, and 4-7PM during the week
- The lifespan of content is eighteen minutes; therefore, you must share blog promotion more than once and on multiple days and different times

3. LinkedIn

- "Post" and "Like"
- Post on group pages, showcase pages, company pages, and in your profile
- Ability to share the post directly through LinkedIn via SlideShare or LinkedIn Plus
- Posts can have up to 600 characters, but only the first 150 are visible in feeds
- Include links and images for the best reactions
- A professional setting that still values engaging and personal content, especially if it asks for readers to interact with the content
- Curate content to appear as a "how-to" for the most opportunity for shares, comments, likes, and post views
- Most frequented times for LinkedIn are 8-10AM and 4-6PM

- Post about once a week
- For content being reshared, change the text a little bit and repost on a different day and time for the best reach

4. Pinterest

- "Pin"
- Images are the most important; the description is only intended to highlight what the post covers
- Pin descriptions can be up to 500 characters, but to get the most activity, keep it between 150 and 300 characters
- Put hashtags in the description to increase searchability
- In the description, add a link to the post and a call-to-action to boost interactions
- Most frequented times for Pinterest are 12-2PM and 7-10PM and all day Saturday and Sunday
- Post the main image the first day of a new blog post and then post additional images spread out throughout the next few weeks after the blog was posted
- Post a few times during the week until all the images are shared
- Instagram
- "Show" and "like"
- Like Pinterest, it is all about the image, but the lifespan is shorter, typically only a few hours
- The image is a square and is 1080 X 1080 pixels
- Captions for images can be up to 2,200 characters, but only the first three lines are visible in the feed, which is typically about 150 characters
- Captions can be solely hashtags because they are so important to the promotion of the post
- The keywords in the blog post make great hashtag options
- Up to 30 hashtags
- Links in captions are not clickable, but it is good practice to include the URL to direct users to your post or blog

- Most frequented times on Instagram are midday and evening Monday through Friday
- Share the main image of your blog on the first day and then share the other images over the following days up to a few weeks after

There are a few ways you can make sharing content across platforms easier for you, especially if you use WordPress. WordPress offers the option of adding a plug-in into your blog site called "Publicize". When you add this to your blog, and you publish a new blog post, you can easily share the content across all the social platforms you set up in the plug-in. It formats the post to best fit with the social media site for you. If you upgrade to a Professional or Premium plan, you can also re-share already published content seamlessly and schedule the social promotion for a certain time. When you tell WordPress to share content through social networks automatically, you will need to log into your social sites when promoted and give them permission to work with your WordPress site. After you set it up, all the work is done for you.

Blogging Trends in 2020

The anticipation of 2020 has already revealed telling information about the future of blogging for this year and even beyond. Below are the trends to look forward to in 2020:

1. Over half of the world's population engages online in some way, and the number is expected to grow.
2. Reading information through blog posts is still steady with more than half the people online reading blogs.
3. Most online interaction, including blog engagement, occurs on a mobile device. More than half of online users engage with content primarily through mobile and spend about 3.5 hours on their mobile phone each day.
4. Most blogs are written in English, on average about 70%, and will continue to be so.

5. Brands are beginning to blog more. Currently, about 55% of all brands blog as a primary marketing strategy and blogging will increase in importance over time.

6. Trust is the focus of blogs, promoting the "truth" rather than the "fake news" on social platforms. Posts will look to build and maintain trust with readers.

7. The story is another important focus of blog posts. People want to hear more personal stories.

8. A video is in demand. More than 85% of traffic searching for information will engage with video in the future.

9. Live video is increasing in popularity and influence others to purchase admissions to an event similar in nature to the live video. Paying to watch a live stream is also an emerging trend.

10. Short content is engaging and giving rise to micro-blogs, sort videos, and simple graphics.

11. Longer posts are still relevant but need to be mixed in with shorter content. Google continues to favor longer content in SEO.

12. Visual content is necessary. Visuals in content all the time is already done by more than 55% of marketers today. In addition, almost 90% of marketers are already using blogs, and they have more than one image in every post. Visuals are expected to grow in importance through the year and about a quarter of all marketers plan to spend more than a quarter of their budget on this alone.

13. Content needs to be interactive to increase engagement. This includes features like quizzes, infographics, and surveys.

14. Content needs to be personalized and relevant to the reader. This is a continuing trend that is unlikely to fade in the long-term future.

15. Partnering with brands and various brands coming together will grow throughout the year.

16. Voice search is increasing in popularity, and capitalizing on this, titles posed as questions will be more important.

17. Visual search is increasing in popularity. Find ways to make your images searchable, such as with embedded links.

18. The focus of blogs is shifted from Millennials to Gen Z, the upcoming "future" generation.

19. A connection is critical. This means having your social accounts all connected to your blog but also the authentic voice you use to connect with your audience. A transparent voice that provides quality content regularly is going to remain in demand.

20. Services for sale are going to increase as partnerships decline. This includes selling workshops, courses, books, etc., to develop a steady revenue stream. However, as mentioned above, the content for sale needs to provide quality to the reader and user.

Chapter 3: Marketing Your Blog

Blog Traffic: The Whys and Hows

When you set out to create a meaningful and profitable blog, you are going to invest a lot of time into it. What you want to know is that this effort is going to be worth it. While there is no guarantee, there are things you can do to help determine if your work is going to bring in the people you need to make the money you want. Bringing people to your blog is the best way to generate revenue. After all, if no one reads your words, no one will pay you for it. So a great measurement for the success of your blog is to monitor how many people visit it. This is called "traffic". The minute you set up your blog, you should be tracking what is coming to it and track it often. One of the benefits of doing this is that you can curate your content to your readers and not waste time on topics they are not engaging with.

You can use analytics tools to help monitor the traffic and how your readers are engaging with your content. These analytical tools identify what posts readers are spending time on and who they are. The analytics also show where on your website your readers are clicking. Using this information, you can spend time on a strategy that is informed. One of the most popular ways to track your blog's traffic and review the analytics is with Google Analytics. Many hosting sites offer their own built-in analytics, but those that do not generally offer a plug-in for Google Analytics. Even if a platform offers its own analytics, you should consider adding in Google Analytics by using the website for it. This is primarily because Google is the monopoly in SEO, so it only makes sense to get their information to improve your blog's performance. In addition, if Google does not recognize your blog, it is going to have a very hard time showing up in front of anyone you are trying to reach.

If you are not sure about how to add Google Analytics to your platform, get onto Google and type in, "How to set up Google Analytics on *insert your platform here. *" Once you get it set up, do not worry if it is a little confusing or intimidating. To begin, start with small checks and balances. Measure a few things just to get the hang of the tool. Once you figure out how the tool works, you are ready to look at the big picture of your blog.

Another important factor to consider is the pages for your blog. Your blog should and probably will naturally end up with more than one page. You will probably start organizing content into different pages like an "About Me" or "Contact" page. You may also chunk up your blog content into different headers and have different kinds of posts that appear on different pages. For example, Lifestyle Bloggers may want to put cooking tips and recipes on one page while DIY tutorials for the home go on another. When you have multiple pages, it is easier for your readers to find your information quickly, but you also need to make sure your analytics are set up to handle this. With Google Analytics, it is easy. This report in Google Analytics is called "All Pages".

The steps to generate this report in Google Analytics are as follows:

    1. Open Google Analytics and log in
    2. Identify the section "Behavior" located in the menu on the left side
    3. Click on "Site Content"
    4. From the options, select "All Pages" to generate the report

Once the report is created, the information will be scattered all around for your pages. You are going to want to filter and move the information around to figure it out. For example, you may not want to gauge the success of your blog on the traffic heading to your "Contact" page. This means you will want to remove this from the results you are seeing. You can remove any page from the report that does not directly relate to your blog. For example, if you have a "Products" page, you can filter them out in relation to the performance of your blog. You can always bring that information back in at a later date if you want to. To filter, the first thing you need to do is determine your blog post URLs. For example, your posts probably have a URL like **www.website.com/blog/post#1**, etc. Every time you create a blog post, "/blog/" is used in the URL. That is what you will use to filter your report by typing it into the "Search" field of the report.

The process of filtering your results is rather simple. You enter the common path or word into your search field and then click on the magnifying glass icon to perform the search. This will then trim down the report to show you data only on the pages that contain that field in the URL. When the report adjusts to your new parameters, the blog posts will be listed out under a nice graph and various metrics listed out for each post.

The metrics in the report are important to understand. Below is a breakdown of what each item means:

1. The first field is the URL for a particular blog post. There is a small square icon in the bottom right corner of the box. This opens the content of the analysis in a new window if you click on it.
2. The second box shows "Pageviews". This tells you how many people have looked at the page during the time frame you told the report to run. For example, if you wanted to see just one day's performance, you can narrow down the report, or you can look at it for the week, month, quarter, or even year.

3. The following column indicates how many people visited the blog post specifically during that same time frame.

4. The average time spent on the page is valuable information. It tells you how long you captured the attention of a reader. Do not get too hung up on this information though. Google can easily misjudge it, especially if you have a high bounce rate.

5. "Entrances" refers to a reader that arrives at your blog post directly. From there, they can engage with your site in another way, like reading another post or visiting another page. This does not refer to a reader that came to your site from somewhere else and then engaged with your blog post.

6. "Bounce Rate", as mentioned earlier in this list, refers to the percentage of readers who entered your site through your blog post directly and then left after engaging in it. These readers do not go to another page or another part of your site after interacting with your specific blog post.

7. "% Exit" is a similar metric, but this refers to the people that came to your blog post from other areas or engaged differently before leaving after engaging with this specific post.

You can use this information to look at the performance of just one blog over a span of time or you can compare your blogs to find certain topics or information that stands out. While this information is very important, you need to recognize that it is not always perfect and accurate. There are always little factors that can throw off your metrics or weirdly skew your data. This means you cannot count on it 100%, but it is the best tool to really gauge what people are doing on your blog.

Now that you understand the information in the "All Pages" report, you need to know how to interpret it. What numbers are "good" and what performance indicators show it is "bad"? This may not be the best way to approach it since all blogs and traffic are different and change drastically over time, but you can start to determine the following:

1. What is the most popular post or posts? Why do you think people liked these specifically? Check comments or contacts you got based on the post to try to put your finger on why your audience engaged with these the most. It could also be the length of the post that was attractive, the topic was trending, it was shared a lot on social media, or it was shared at a specific time. See if you can find something that stands out, especially if you are looking at a couple of popular posts. What is common about the two of them that you think made them more popular than the rest?

2. How can you use this information to develop a content strategy around these successful traits? If you see that your most popular posts are ones that have a short video clip and are about 500 words, can you replicate this format more often? Or were your posts shared by readers on social media after you posted on Facebook at 4 PM on a Wednesday? Can you make sure your promotion strategy includes posting at this time more often in the future?

3. In addition, you can play with your posts that are successful by adjusting or updating them in some way. This can potentially get more life from the post and show you valuable information about what your audience is interested in. For example, if a popular post is already successful, what if you added more information to it or an integrative feature, like a survey or quiz? Can you see an increase in activity again or do your readers move on?

4. Look at the length of time between your popular posts. Is there a certain amount of time between the two that you could replicate? If you increased the number of posts in a certain time frame, which means you post more frequently, do you increase traffic to your blog? If you find a "sweet spot" for frequency, can you keep up that frequency long

term? To determine this, sit down and look at your calendar. Be realistic or even overestimate how much time it will take for you to create a post. Can you do this every week? There will be more information on this later; however, it is good to start considering it now.

Beginning to understand your blog's traffic and what it means to your future strategy is vital to your growth and success. This introduction is just to "get your feet wet"; however, you can begin to formulate your approach to understanding the performance of your blog and how you plan on using your metrics to reach your audience better.

Social Media Is Your (Marketing) Friend

You want your blog to generate traffic. This means you want to use social media to your advantage. People congregate on sites like Facebook and Twitter more than any other place on the Internet. When they are looking for information, one of the first places they start is through a social media outlet. It is also where these people share their opinions and experiences openly. The people you want to reach are probably on one or more of these sites regularly. This means it is an ideal location to launch a marketing strategy. Instead of hoping that people eventually find your blog, you can design advertisements and strategy to connect with your audience.

To help you in general when using social media for promotion, consider the following tips that can be applied to just about any form of social media:

1. Always add a link to your posts. Get in the habit of always linking people back to your blog, even if your post is not about a recent blog post. This leads people from your quipping posts to your content-rich blog topics.
2. On your blog are social buttons linking to your various social media pages. At least have a link to Facebook. Add other social media platforms that you use regularly. This

leads people to follow you through social media and not just through your blog.

3. Enable others to share your blogs on social media. Most platforms have an easy feature you can add to your blog site to promote sharing of your content across a variety of social platforms.

4. Include a clickable link in your blog post to your social media. In addition, if you have a video on YouTube that you want your readers to engage with, embed the video directly into your post, right in the middle, so they can easily see it when they load your blog post.

The last suggestion brings up a good topic to review briefly; using video in your blog posts. It is a growing medium and influencer. Many people still discredit YouTube as a social media site, but it really does fall into this category. In general, because of its ability to share visual information with anyone, it is one of the most popular social media sites. Often, the majority of the video you find on other sites is cut from YouTube or can be found in a longer form on YouTube. In addition to embedding video in your blog posts, you can embed your video in a Facebook post easily. The platforms work nicely together, and the process is pretty seamless. It is a valuable tool that can be easily maximized and provides evergreen content.

Taking the time to develop your content marketing strategy through social media is worth the time and effort. You have to compete with all the other information out there, and having a strong plan on how you will do it will help you stand out from the crowd. You can also boost your impact on different platforms that already have a huge audience with constant views. Below are suggestions on how to plan an effective strategy for social media and your blog:

1. *Offer a teaser and boost it.* On Facebook, you can hint about what your upcoming blog is going to be about. Once you create the post, you then pay to boost it to a wider audience. This option allows you to pay for the engagement you get but only up to the dollar amount you are prepared to

spend and for the length of time you want it to run for. Your boosted post can include anything from words to a video. Develop anything that you think will attract the attention of your audience and get them wanting your upcoming blog post.

2. *When you post a video on YouTube, add your blog's homepage link in the description of the video.* If your video is related to your blog post directly, add a link in the video and a recorded call-to-action asking people to go there.

3. *Create cross-links on different platforms.* For whatever reason, people seem to hesitate about cross-linking content. It may be from past algorithms in Google, but in reality, Google has never cared about cross-linking as long as it is above board and the content is pertinent to one another. You can also bring people from one platform to the next to learn more about a certain subject or expand information on a topic.

4. *Create fresh content daily on Twitter and even Facebook.* The more often you post, the more hype you can generate. Of course, the content needs to be valuable, but also short. If you can keep posts fun and easy to engage with, people are more likely to enjoy them. Instead of posting a long post on Facebook, for example, consider chunking up the information into little bites that you can share over a few days.

5. Now and then, offer a giveaway. This attracts people to your blog and your social accounts. Most social media users like to get something for free when they read or engage with your material. The main objective of this strategy should be to offer quality content, but the secondary objective should be to show that you appreciate their readership and loyalty. Most of the time, the free item you choose to giveaway does not need to be elaborate or expensive. Offering an eBook or something digital like a checklist of some sort can be just as valuable to your readers as something physical.

6. Do not discount less-popular social media sites in your strategy. Using social media for marketing does not mean you are exempt from the social part of it. People go to social media for more personal interaction, not to engage with business marketing messages. This means you need to show people the personal side of your money-making blog, like you doing things, your family, adventures you have been on, etc. This can be done well through the less popular social media accounts for marketing, such as Instagram. The influence of Instagram as a marketing platform is evolving, but it is still not the most commonly used platform. To capitalize on this platform for your blog posts and connect to your audience, consider adding images of personal pictures related to your blog and your life. For example, if you are a food blogger, post pictures of the great food you have made or eaten, and also the not-so-great experiences or attempts. Show people you "polished" and present something amazing, but also a picture of your kitchen after a photo shoot and the mountain of dishes and things needing to be cleaned up. This approach helps show readers what your company is all about and establishes a stronger sense of connection that other platforms may not be the best for.

Pinterest Marketing in More Detail

If you noticed earlier in this book the mention of different types of blogs that benefit from promotion on Pinterest, you will probably realize how important it is to use it to your advantage for just about any type of blog you are creating. To help you start thinking about a strong Pinterest marketing strategy, consider the following for 2020:

1. Be consistent and regular. Like other sites, make sure you put out valuable content regularly. To help you stay on a regular schedule, consider using a service like Tailwind. This way you avoid feat-and-famine pinning and can keep your followers happy and content.

2. *Do not "repin" content to boost it in Pinterest again.* Instead, repost information from your blog again, so it is a fresh pin. Fresh and new content is favored in Pinterest in 2020, so this is the best strategy to get your content out there again without having to come up with new content over and over again.

3. *One source, many pins.* One blog can generate many fresh pinning opportunities. Make sure, with each pin, that is has a unique description. This is best for optimizing SEO and the Smart Feed algorithm on Pinterest. You can also change the landing image of an older post and create a new pin to that source. This helps reinvigorate the content without having to rewrite information.

4. *Get seasonal content out in advance.* People use Pinterest to get ideas about upcoming events, such as holidays or times of the year. For example, people start thinking about decorating for fall and back to school in late July. This means you should be getting your seasonal content up about 45 days before the holiday or event. You can create new pins for content you have already created or generate new content in advance for fresh traffic.

5. *Do not neglect your boards.* The name you choose for your boards is searchable. This means you should be choosing names that have keywords in them and a strong SEO. Also, sections on Pinterest will probably become more important in the future for searches so add a section if it is relevant to your boards.

6. *The people you follow and that follow you are important.* It is good to follow people that offer engaging content that is relevant to your blog and your audience. In addition, make sure to encourage people not just to follow you on Pinterest, but to repin your content and add valuable contributions to the site. The more engagement you get on this site, the better. It is not always about the numbers.

7. *Make your posts pinnable.* Make it simple and obvious that your readers can and should pin your content on Pinterest for you. Anyone who engages with your blog post should know that you are active on Pinterest, what images you are encouraged to pin, and how to do it easily. You can even guide them in what to say when they pin your content!

8. *Link your other social media accounts to Pinterest.* There are other visually-centered social media platforms out there, such as Instagram and even YouTube. Now you can connect them and easily share content from one to the other. And you do not need to be the one sharing it! Linking the accounts makes it easier for your audience to pin from another social site onto Pinterest. This boosts your engagement and increases your impressions and visibility. In addition, it opens up more reach for your audience and shows your readers that you are in more places for them to engage with. If they thought you were only posting a video on YouTube, but then learn you are on Pinterest, you can get them to engage more through Pinterest too. And it can work the other way around! People from Pinterest can then be exposed to your blog, Instagram, Etsy, LinkedIn, etc.

Leads and Lists: How They Work

To begin, you need to know a few things, like what exactly is a "lead", "lead generation", and "mailing list". For some of you, this may sound intuitive. For others, you may have no idea what in the world those are referring to, and even for others, you may think you know what they mean, but as you read through the definitions, you may become surprised at what you learn. Here are some short descriptions to help you before diving into the information further:

- *Leads*: Potential readers or "buyers". These people have shown an interest in some area of your blog or online presence and have willingly shared contact information with you so you can communicate more directly with them.

• *Lead Generation*: Opportunity for potential "buyers or "engagers" to share their contact information with you when they express interest in your blog or presence online. This is how you get people to give you more direct contact methods for future communication.

• *Mailing List*: The compilation of all the contact information leads have shared with you. This is how you organize the information they have shared with you and how you can contact them directly in the future more easily than trying to find a form or document with information written on it. Think of a spreadsheet with names, phone numbers, email addresses, etc. You can add information on here about how they interacted or showed interest in your online content so you can easily tailor messages to them.

Now that you know what they are, how do they really add value to your blog and making money? Here is a quick breakdown of that information for each one:

• *Leads*: People are not responsive to the "cold call". They do not want to talk with someone on the phone or in person unless they know it is valuable. However, online is another story. People are willing to engage with others online because it is less "risky". Because more people are willing to connect online, you can reach more people and people that are often hard to "catch" in person. Bringing more people to your site means more engagement. More engagement means more opportunity to make money through PPC, etc. In addition, more traffic to your blog means more opportunity for partnerships, etc.

• *Lead Generation*: Generating opportunity for leads and potential loyal readers are how you have new people to talk to. It is a fresh perspective and allows a new group of people to buy your book or sign up with the online course you created. It is how you bring people to your blog and interact with your posts. You can employ very strategic targeting methods to get the "right" types of leads for your blog instead of just putting out a message somewhere online in the hope of reaching the best people.

• *Mailing List*: There is no point in gathering all these potential readers and loyal followers if you do not talk with them. It is also not wise to gather all this information and not organize it in an easy-to-use manner. When you create a mailing list, you improve the way you can reach and communicate with those that are interested in what you have to say. This improves the quality of what you have to offer and whom you are offering it to.

Now that you know how important leads, lead generation, and mailing lists are for your social media strategy, here are several methods for generating these leads for your blog traffic and money-making success:

1. **If you want to be really savvy, create some content that is not readily available to just any visitor.** This is called "gated" content. Think of it like being hidden on your blog behind an invisible, electronic gate. Only the people with the "key" can get in to see it. The "key" in this instance is a special link or password. If they think the information you are offering to share is valuable and important enough to them, they are going to share their information with you to get access to it. The price of "admissions" is typically his or her name and basic contact information, like an email address. You can also lead people to a landing page that instructs them to put in his or her information to get access. Those that are only mildly interested will leave, but those that are still curious will exchange their information to get "in". The people willing to put in their information are the leads worth following up with. To turn your social media followers into blog engagers can be as simple as offering gated content to them. This content can be just about

anything, and you should try out a few different options to see what people respond to the most.

2. **Challenge your followers with a contest.** Make sure the prize for completing the contest is something your followers are interested in and valuable to those that have the best potential of becoming your loyal readers. This is important because people will not engage in your contest if they do not see value in the prize at the end, but it is most valuable to the people who will follow your blog loyally (and even buy your products in the future—if you decide to sell something). Remember: your contest needs to target your ideal reader. If you gather a whole bunch of leads and information, but it is not useful, it can feel like a waste of time. Instead, take some time to figure out the best reward for the people you want to stick around. Good examples of prizes include a free upgrade, a sample of a product, or access to an online workshop or training for free. These are things that you already offer that people who are most valuable to your blog would be interested in already. You can have people "enter" the challenge a few different ways; by following, liking, sharing, retweeting, tagging a specific post, or by clicking on a certain link leading to an attractive landing page. Having someone follow, like, share, etc., on social media is simple and effective. The challenge, however, is that people are then only sharing publicly available information. Also, if you do this a lot, Facebook especially, will tag your posts as spam and decrease your distribution. Asking your followers to take an extra step to go to a landing page means fewer people participating, but you can get more information, especially if you guide them to a "contest entry form" where they have to share lead information.

3. **Use the advertising options on various social media sites.** Especially being new to blogging and capturing leads, take advantage of the tools set up to help you. Yes, eventually you will learn different tips and tricks that are

more advanced, but this is still one of the best methods for gathering quality leads for your mailing list. This is probably one of the best and easiest ways to target a clear group of people effectively. Facebook is an excellent platform for this, but you can also do this effectively through LinkedIn and Instagram.

4. Offer an online live video, webinar, or hangout to generate more valuable leads. Webinars are one of the most valuable options to offer; however, you can leverage other options as well to bring people together and gather contact information. You can combine this tip with the idea of "gated" content, making people enter their contact information before they can access the video or hangout, or open the content to everyone but use the event to gather leads by encouraging participation (comments and other forms of engagement during the webinar or live video) with the reward of an attractive prize to the most engaged or by leading people to another spot on your blog for them to get a discount or more details about a contest you are running.

If these ideas seem overwhelming or intimidating, just make sure you have a place on every page of your blog for people to sign up for a "newsletter" or "special updates" from you. This way, when you post a new blog or want to share information with them, they can be in the loop. Having a pop-up on your site is good, or you can just have a place on each page with a button asking them to "stay connected" with you. This is not the most proactive way, but it is a simple and good approach to make sure you are asking people to stay loyal to your information and solutions.

SEO in 2020: Dos and Don'ts

SEO is not what it used to be. You can no longer easily spam the Internet and trick your way into the top ranks of search engines. Yes, there is still "spamdexing". This means manipulating indexes or search engine algorithms to increase SEO. Sometimes, this means link building or stringing a whole bunch of unrelated phrases together to rank higher. The risk of doing something like this is that Google will flag your blog and penalize for inappropriate processes. One of the processes Google has put in place is called Google Penguin. This algorithm is designed specifically to find people trying to manipulate the guidelines set forth by the search engine. This is great for users, but not great for those wanting to get good SEO ranking quickly by non-valuable means. This development now forces you to be a bit more strategic about your methods, which in the long run is great for your blog and the money you can make.

"SEO" is an acronym for "Search Engine Optimization". The "better" your SEO, the higher on the search engine list you get. Over time and experience, the process for determining SEO has improved, but it has always been present. In order to generate "good" SEO, you need to do certain things and avoid others. Below is a breakdown of some of the most important "dos" and "don'ts" of SEO for your blog:

The "Dos":

1. *Evaluate how your blog is performing with the help of analytical tools, such as Google Analytics.* This was introduced earlier and is so important that it bears repeating. Part of this process is making sure you research keywords and choose options that are relevant, popular, but not oversaturated. As you continue to read on, notice that keywords and the importance of choosing these wisely pop up time and time again.

2. *Use descriptive text to your advantage.* This also includes using keywords wisely. Especially when you are describing your blog, make sure those 55 words are well chosen. The main text for your blog description is called "Meta text" and is what you are using to attract your readers. The "tags" you choose are snippets of text that add more detail to "what" your blog is all about. Your tags need to be clear and relevant. Precision and specificity are critical. Each tag needs

to be unique, and the keywords should not be drawn out and lengthy.

3. *Insert internal links often.* You can add links in your description to help improve your SEO. Link keywords that are connected to your blog and content-wise, but choose only one internal link with a good quality keyword. If you get wild and put many internal links in a single post, you will destroy your SEO. Google considers multiple links that lead to the same place as spam and will penalize you for it.

4. *Images not only visually support your content, but also help your SEO.* Any graphics, charts, or images you put in it boost the quality of your content. While Google does not directly "see" the images in your post, it does "read" the links and tags attached to the images. Images should also have unique keywords associated with it, also revealing the quality of your post to Google. In addition, while putting "long-tail" keywords in your general blog description, you can add them to your images without penalty.

5. *Choose content that users can engage with easily.* This is also called "user-friendly" content. If you say your blog and posts will deliver something, make sure it does just that. Make sure that your visitors have a positive experience, and try to get them to stay on your site for a while by creating an easy-to-use blog site and valuable content. If they stay for a while and look around, your bounce rate lowers and your SEO increases. On the other hand, not delivering what you say you will or offering little to no value means a higher bounce rate of visitors and thereby lowering your SEO.

6. *Do not forget the importance of mobile.* A large majority of people engage with blogs and online content through a mobile device. If you are not set up to accommodate mobile viewing, you are going to get a hit to your SEO in favor of those that can deliver a good mobile experience.

7. *Use a map for your blog, even if it is just a couple of pages.* Google does not like a site that does not have an

attached site map. If you are using a host and template, most likely, this is already included for you. If you are breaking out and designing your own, make sure to include one on there for your SEO alone.

The "Don'ts":

1. *Copy content directly from another website.* It is very easy for SEO algorithms to identify content that is not fresh and that has been copied and pasted in another place. If it is done too blatantly or you do this often, your SEO will be extremely low.

2. *You have an external link overload.* Having too many links out from your blog is spamming, and Google will flag it fast. In addition, if your viewers do not find the links you are sharing relevant or functional, your bounce rate will increase, also lowering your SEO. Instead, stick to internal links and just a few external links with relevant keywords.

3. *Links or text is hidden in your content.* This is an old trick that used to work but now is a major "faux pas". Most of the time, this is used for malicious purposes; mainly to hide viruses and malware in posts or pages. While it could boost your posts and blog for a bit, it can run the risk of having your blog being banned from Google. It is really not worth the risk!

4. *Content is only test-focused.* Readers get bored with just words. They need a little visual stimulation. You can also add interest in call-outs and highlighted quotes to help break up the text. Doing this means readers stay longer, which helps your SEO.

5. *Each post has the same or a very similar heading.* While this can help boost your SEO, it will confuse and annoy your readers. This, in turn, will increase your bounce rate and hurt your SEO in the long run.

6. *Links to other websites are included with abandon and little research.* If Google has penalized a website for a certain

reason and you link to them, you could be unknowingly hurting yourself. In addition, if you link to a website with adult content, you could be damaging your blog and its SEO. If you do insert links to other sites or blogs, make sure you are doing so carefully and with a good understanding of the opportunity and risk.

Paid vs. Free Traffic

You can pay people to visit your site, or you can find ways to get them there for free. Both have their advantages, but both have their disadvantages too. Many successful, money-making bloggers choose to do a combination of the two, but the balance between paid and free is up to you. Paying for traffic means buying ads, mailing lists, etc. Anything that requires you to pay for it to reach or target an audience is considered a paid traffic generator. On the other hand, using resources, like social media's free resources, is a way to generate traffic without investing money. This does not necessarily make it "free", however, because the tradeoff is often a larger investment of time and energy. Below is a generic list of paid or free ideas to help drive more traffic to your blog:

1. Focus on developing and managing a quality mailing list.
2. Guest blog on other's sites to bring people back to your blog too.
3. Focus on improving your SEO as outlined in the previous section.
4. Come up with a plan to reach out to other bloggers to help you promote your content. They will probably do the same to you in the future. This is a win-win.
5. Follow other bloggers and post engaging and relevant comments on their posts.
6. Ask other bloggers to share your content, especially if you feature them in your post.
7. Create a post with a roundup of experts on a certain topic. Ask "experts" in a certain field or on a certain topic to offer their advice on a subject and tag them in the post.

8. Develop a list of valuable resources for your readers for a specific niche or topic.

9. Interview influential people and outline your discussion and takeaways from the conversation. Make sure to tag the person you interviewed and ask them to share the content with their followers too.

10. Run a contest.

11. Create a strategy for social media based on your analytics.

12. Always include social sharing buttons on your posts and your site.

13. Create and share infographics for your niche.

14. Creates slides to share on SlideShare for another reach.

15. Join relevant Facebook groups to your niche and post catchy and graphic-focused posts regularly.

16. Seek out opportunities to be interviewed or speak on podcasts.

17. Cover major events with your niche's perspective in mind.

18. Do not shy away from controversy. Be firm in an opinion, make a strong argument, and invite people to share their opinions and perspectives. Open a dialogue that is productive, not attacking. It is risky but "hot".

19. Stay transparent and clear while offering value to your readers.

20. Start a podcast related to your blog.

21. Advertise on sites like Reddit or Facebook or StumbleUpon.

22. Create a challenge for blogging or sponsor one.

23. Offer a giveaway.

24. Join your local HARO group. This is a site that connects "sources" or "stories" to local reporters. Reporters are always looking for people to interview and you can be just one of those experts they meet with. If they use your information or

words in a story, make sure to ask that they publish your blog link too.

25. Spend time working on your strategy for your site map, email and signature responses, and keyword research. Creating a plan or strategy for maximizing these things frees up your time to stay focused on delivering quality content that counts.

Socializing, Commenting, and Being Heard

It can be isolating when you first enter the world of blogging. You can feel like you are turning from a real person with a passion into this Internet being churning out words and images for deep space. Try not to lose yourself in this process. You are a human being with a need for social connection. Blogging is an excellent method for developing this connection with no geographic, economic, etc., boundaries. The more you get out from your blog and engage with others, the stronger you build your blogger friendships and connections, but you also strengthen your individuality as a blogger. This is personal business, so make sure you stay connected to this.

It may sound enticing and easy to add a quick, meaningless comment to another blogger's post with a link to your blog. In that context, yes it is, but if you want to be professional and not get tagged for spamming, you need to add value to the discussion with your post, as well as your backlink to your blog or specific blog post. For example, instead of saying something like, "Great topic! John Doe, **www.johndoeblog.com**," try adding a comment like, "Wow, I like your stance on sustainability in fashion. Very bold! How do you see large corporate companies embracing this concept over making money? I'm curious about how you would approach that conversation! Thanks for sharing. John Doe, **www.johndoeblogs.com**." This type of comment opens up the opportunity to connect and engage with the other blogger in a meaningful way. The first example offers no opportunity for connection or content.

Try to avoid adding comments for the sake of adding comments and stay away from things like,

- "Nice post!"
- "Amazing share!"
- "Great details!"

Instead of wasting your time on this meaningless commentary, try the following:

1. Use Gravatar to add an image to your profile used for commenting on blogs.
2. When you read another bloggers' posts, try to figure out how you can add value to their information.
3. If you liked the post enough to share it on your social media channels, let the blogger know in the comments section. This is a sign of respect and appreciation for a job well done.

Chapter 4: Monetizing Your Blog

Monetizing Your Blog Like A Pro

Making money from your blog, your voice, and your words are possible, but it is not simple. It is not an easy process, especially if you are looking to make money rather than just play around as a Hobbyist. The fact remains that online marketing is necessary for the success of your blog and your income. There are basics you need to know and follow in order for this to happen. The purpose of this chapter is to offer these basics to you in a way that is clear and foundational. This way you can use the information to grow and develop alongside your blog. It is truly the best way to monetize your blog as a professional blogger.

There are five "laws" you must obey for a successful blog. Following these laws will lead to long-term success. Ignoring them will make your life harder, and your blog will struggle to find the success you desire. The fives laws are:

1. Focus
2. Quality
3. Value
4. Engagement
5. Authority

First, you need a niche. You need to have a clear focus on your content and your audience. Do not try to be all things to everyone or spread your content out all over the place. Even Lifestyle bloggers have a series of topics that they regularly cover for their targeted niche. You want a "core" full of loyal and engaged readers. If you start veering off on topics that are not related to them, you start to lose their interest, and therefore, start to lose their loyalty. The best way to solve your audience's problems is to stay on topic.

Your topic needs to be valuable to your audience, not just to you. Value comes in the form of a well-researched and well-written piece of content that has sources, links, and in-depth knowledge. The more quality you offer in a single post, the better. Quality is always better than quantity in the world of blogging. This value teaches, instructs, guides, and delivers to your audience. Think tutorials, infographics, etc., designed just for your niche. People learn in different ways, so include different ways to reach people with the same message. For example, some people love and thrive by reading about something, while visuals are better for others. In addition, hearing content is another method people learn best. This means having text, images, and a short video in a single post can be a powerful tool to reach more people. You do not need to do this every time, but it is a good idea to remember this when developing your content and promo strategy.

When you create content that people value and you are obviously aiming to help your audience more than focus on yourself, you have a greater chance of engaging them. The more people engage and spend time on your content, the more money you can make. You can make this money by selling your products or through other monetization strategies. The fact is: the more people that spend more time on your content means the more you can make. They are not going to engage in your content that does not have focus, quality, or value, so make sure to check those boxes off first before trying to get people to interact with your posts. And when you have those first three things checked off, you also have a better chance at the fifth "law"; authority. If you are not already considered an expert or authority in your niche, your amazing posts will start developing that reputation for you. The stronger your reputation as a leader in this niche is, the better the opportunity for engaging an audience and making money you will have. This is called "leveraging" your influence, and there is nothing wrong with it as long as you keep the first three points in mind every time.

These "laws" were covered in the previous chapters; so hopefully, they are not "new news". But now that you understand the link between all of them and the importance of each, you can now focus on how to turn these laws into profits. There are generally eight different ways you can make money through blogging. Not all the methods are best for all types of blogs, but once you review the details of each, you can decide which ones to use for the niche you are targeting. Of course, there are always new and different methods for making money through your blog. As you read through this review of the "Core Eight", you may find yourself thinking, "Yeah, but what about..." The purpose of this is to introduce you to the major monetization methods that typically span across various types of blogs well. They are the "foundation" of money making through blogs. All the other ones that pop up are great, and maybe your bread-and-butter monetization in the future. However, for now, these are a great place to start:

1. Affiliate marketing

This is a big one. The biggest and most popular possibly. When you start out, this is one of the best things to leverage. Most likely, in the beginning, you do not have things to sell, so this method is great to start generating revenue. Just make sure that your content matches the affiliate promotion; for example, if you are writing about yoga, promoting affiliates links for yoga accessories like jewelry, home décor, and other accessories is a good avenue for your audience.

2. Advertisements (Ads)

PPC, or "Pay Per Click", is a popular method and something you can easily add to your blog; however, the income does not really start pouring in from this method until you reach between 10,000 and 100,000 visitors each day. This is a lot of expectations for a new blog and blogger. Instead, contact advertisers and seek to negotiate set terms for including their relevant advertisements on your blog. Remember: relevant. Most likely, doing this will bring you more money in the beginning than PPC ads would.

3. Market through email using your mailing list

Build your mailing list and send out regular emails. This is a powerful money-making method. You can use any one of the email marketing platforms out there to help you. While your email may not make money, the connection and loyalty you create will. People will be more likely to engage with your content and buy your products if you are connecting them to information that is valuable to them. A good estimate is to view each new mailing list subscriber as about $1 profit for you.

4. Sell eBooks, White Papers, etc.

Develop a book or an in-depth paper that digs in deeper regarding the content on your blog, and you can sell it to your readers looking for more. You can easily develop a non-fiction digital book that can teach and guide people more than just a simple post can do. Once you create your book, promote it on your blog and through social media. You can use this also to help generate leads and develop your mailing list. As you grow, look into a way to sell your book on autopilot, so it is a great form of passive income for you.

5. Sell workshops, courses, etc.

Like books, you can sell online training. If you can create training that is valuable and well researched, you can sell them for a decent amount of money. You should not think of your effort put into these as quick, done-in-an-hour-and-then-make-a-ton-of-money type courses. You need to put a lot of time and effort into creating an amazing workshop or course for your readers. Once you put in this effort, though, you should be able to sell them easily for a long time. Technical skills tend to work well as courses and workshops, but you can probably find a way to train someone on other topics like fitness, health, and fashion. A good goal is to find what is already being offered as a course in that niche and then come up with something even more valuable.

6. Sell digital products

You may not want or be able to set the time aside to write a book or record a stellar workshop or course right now. That does not mean that you cannot sell something valuable to your readers. Any digital item that is valuable to your readers can be sold for a profit. Think about a checklist or worksheet that your readers could benefit from. Digital content comes in many forms, including videos and PDFs. Find a gap in things your readers could use and put it out there. You will be surprised at the amount of money you can make offering a digital product like a checklist or training video.

7. Offer to coach your readers digitally

Just about everyone is offering to coach others in some form or another. While "everyone" is already doing it, you can profit from this too. You can coach people on healthy eating, living a good life, making money, succeeding in business, etc. Choose a topic you are knowledgeable about and can offer as a real service to your niche and develop a training program. You can make a significant chunk of money through just a few clients this way. Make sure when you do this that you cap the number of clients you are willing to take on at a time and answer questions or discuss concerns before getting started. Also, keep the transaction and interactions simple. The more complicated the process to sign up and get coached, the less likely you will have a steady stream of coaching clients.

8. Sponsorships

Like affiliate links and advertisements, this one relies on traffic. The more people you get to visit your blog, the more money you can make through sponsorships. Sponsored posts are great, but you need to be transparent about the sponsorship to your readers. You can get penalized if you are trying to pass off a sponsorship as "organic" and personally-driven content. It is not worth trying to hide the fact that you were paid or sponsored to write the review or post, so make it very clear what is going on in the post. Your readers will appreciate the transparency and Google will be accepting of your content.

Now that you are introduced to the different core methods for making money through your blog, it is time to dig a little bit deeper into each topic for you.

1. Affiliate Marketing

As a new blogger, affiliate marketing is a great way to start earning a little bit of money. There are several tips to help you get the most out of your efforts and to provide value to your readers better. First, choose just a handful of products or services to target. You can get carried away promoting, promoting, promoting, but your readers do not want to see a whole list of affiliate links and nothing of fresh perspective. The best bet is to choose a couple of things you are really passionate about and that you think can really help your readers, and aggressively promote those. This creates a cornerstone of your income through affiliate marketing. You can introduce other affiliate links that support blog topics or other content, even the main affiliate links you are promoting, but you need a couple that is your core.

Focusing on a handful of opportunity helps you focus on making money from them specifically. When you are thinking about your content for your next blog post, how can you integrate one or more of your cornerstone affiliates products or services? You can even use this to help design the layout of your next blog post. Even your email marketing can be influenced by the affiliate links. To get the most out of your affiliate marketing, make sure you can check off the majority of the following points:

- You have used the product or service in the past and know it is valuable personally.
- The product or service is very relevant to the majority of your niche, and it will interest most of them.
- The financial benefit of promoting this product or service is worth it. This does not mean it has to be a high payout, but that would be nice. It just needs to offer you something that makes promoting it worthwhile to you.

Once you choose your affiliate products or services, figure out where you are going to promote them. You only make money when a person clicks on the link and buys something. This means you need to put it where your niche will see it and take action. Great places to consider are on headers, in blog post content, listed at the end of a post, or even a section that leads into a post. Sidebars do not get much attention. Most readers ignore this spot because they know it is an advertisement. Instead, find a place that is obvious and prominent.

One of the most effective places to place an affiliate link is in an email. Your mailing list is a great place to start promoting your affiliations. Every email should not include a product or service promotion, but it can occasionally, and your email subscribers will be more likely to purchase something if they find your content valuable and trust your advice. You can develop trust through a valuable email marketing strategy and occasionally throw in an email with affiliate products in there. To succeed in this arena, constantly grow and enhance your email mailing list and marketing plan. Choosing an email marketing platform to help you maintain your mailing list and sending out customized content to your readers can also help you with having auto-responses set up to help promote your affiliate products. For example, no matter when a person subscribes, you can have a series of set emails that get out to them with content that you curate. One of more of those auto-response emails can include promotion of your affiliate links. For example, when a person subscribes, they get a series of ten introductory emails. Each one is spaced out to be sent a few days apart from one another, and the content is designed to be valuable and connected to their interests. The emails should have links to the products you are promoting and also back to your blog for more details. Once you set this up, the email marketing provider does all the work, bringing your mailing list back again and again to your blog with no more effort from you.

Hopefully, you have come to realize that just sticking a banner ad on the top of your blog is not going to cut it. Most affiliate programs offer banner ads for your site, and you should not completely discredit them, but they are not going to be how you generate the most sales from your affiliations. The reasons businesses are even offering affiliations are for a more organic appearance and personalized promotion of their products. Banner ads make it look like a paid advertisement, and this is not effective for you or them. Instead of relying only on banner ads, promote the products and services in different ways, like in blog content and email messages as mentioned earlier. Even publishing an entire post about the product and reviewing your experiences with it can be helpful. Make sure this review is honest and personal. Share the good and the bad in it. You can be honest that you receive monetary compensation for promoting the product or service, but that your review is your personal experience with the affiliation, and also, it is why you are promoting it in the first place.

If you write a review, or even if you do not, consider writing a post about how to use the product or service. Offer a tutorial with tips and suggestions on how to get the most out of it. Show readers how you integrate the affiliation in your personal life. This not only promotes the product but shows your readers how it can help them as it has helped you. Posting content in this way is a bit more organic and can also help in SEO. Consider adding posts like this to your auto-responder strategy so you can help your readers and generate affiliate income.

Also, make sure your evergreen posts have affiliate links in them somewhere or some way. You can also go back and add links to these key posts. If you add information to your older, high-performing posts, launch a new promotion strategy for them. Push the info back out through social media channels and link it in and to newer content that you have published. You can also guide people to these posts with the help of a "start here" landing page for new visitors. This homepage guides people to the top performing posts as well as content promoting your affiliate links. This is a great way to guide people right away to moneymakers for you and helpful content for them. When your readers find your promotions and affiliations valuable to them, you can ask them also to share your content with their network. This is essentially readers sharing your content to get you more exposure and money. Use resources like Social Locker, Just Retweet, and Viral Content Buzz to assist you.

Finally, do not be afraid to ask affiliate companies to give you more commission for promoting their content. If you are constantly promoting one or two different products and are generating a lot of sales for them, it is normal and acceptable to ask for a higher commission. It is common to receive a higher commission than what is advertised, especially if you have a track record of successful affiliate promotion. Companies pay more to keep top performers and also keep business away from their competition. When you ask for more commissions, have a strong case to justify the higher payout. This means being able to share your track record of success and how you are more effective than the average blogger with your strategy. You do not need to share details of your strategy, but you can show how your approach generates sales for the company, and this is what the whole purpose is for their affiliate program.

2. Ads

Contacting advertisers to have direct ads on your blog is a great and easy method for generating income. PPC is another method. Many bloggers rely on Google AdSense to help them make money through ads, but there are many other methods to consider and add to your blog in addition to Google AdSense. Below is a breakdown of different advertising methods to consider for your blog:

- *PPC*: Also called CPC or "Cost per Click". This just means that an advertiser will give you money for each click on the ad that they get from your blog. Advertisers like this include Infolinks, Media.net, and Chitika. Most of the time, you get your payout once you hit your minimum limits, such as $50 or $100, depending on the payout method you choose and the provider you choose to work with.

- *Sell ad space:* This is probably more financially beneficial for new blogs, but an advertiser needs to see that you are already bringing in a decent amount of traffic to make it worth it for them. If you offer ad space on your blog, develop a page for "Advertising with Us". This way, advertisers can go there to learn about how you plan to share their information and how much it costs them each month. This is also the place to share why it is valuable for them to pay to advertise with you. This includes rankings on Google, Alexa, etc. You can also use services for selling ad space on your blog too. For example, BuySellAds and BlogAds sell your ad space and take a percentage of the profits for their efforts. Most of the time, these companies will only work with established blogs with good traffic so make sure you get your page views and visitors up to use this type of service.

- *Offer text links for sale on your blog:* It is kind of like selling ad space, but be careful with this method. It is vital that you offer the "Nofollow" tag on the text link, so you do not get penalized from Google. Linkworth is a common provider for text links and offers a minimum payout between $25 and $100.

- *CPM:* Instead of being paid when a reader clicks on an ad, you are paid by the impressions. Instead of being paid with a click, when you have a certain number of visitors, you get paid a set amount. This means, for example, that you get $500 when 100,000 people see the ad. PulsePoint is a common option for CPM. It is important that you have a lot of original and fresh content often and decent traffic in order to capitalize on this option.

- *Pop-Ups:* Many people, bloggers, marketers, and readers alike do not like pop-ups. While they are not a popular option, it is still something you can consider. Thankfully, with many advertisers, you can choose how often you want the pop-up appearing on your site as well as your price. PopAds is a good option to consider for this type of advertisement.

- *Paid reviews:* This is not necessarily a traditional advertisement, but it is advertising a product for a company that you are paid to offer a review for. For example, if the company sends you a product to try out and write a piece for, you could receive anywhere between $150 and $500 as compensation. This does depend on your niche, traffic, and rank. Some companies will offer their own independent offers, or you can go through a resource like PayU2Blog or SponsoredReviews. The great thing about being paid to write reviews is that you do not need to write only positive content. The original, personal, and honest discussion of the products is what the companies are looking for through this method of advertising.

3. Selling digital products (eBooks, white papers, checklists, worksheets, etc.)

Digital products, also sometimes called "information products", refer to any type of digitally-based content that provides information and value to a customer. You can offer a video, eBook, audio recording, checklist, etc. A digital product is anything that has a tangible aspect. This means it does not include services like webinars, courses, coaching, and memberships. Those topics will be covered later in this chapter because they need a slightly different approach to making money and promotion.

This biggest difference between offering free content through your blog and selling digital content like a book or video is that you are offering more than just information; you are offering solutions and techniques to improve their lives. You are a guide and resource for their future advancement and growth. Your digital products need to bring that to them in more depth than your posts offer. You can offer other physical products, like a printed book, DVD, or other products, but for the interest of this section, the products discussed here are all digitally based. Those topics will be covered later in this chapter. The advantage of offering a digital product is that you do not need to pay and store inventory and then deal with shipping and delivery methods. Digital content offers immediate access for your customers and no major efforts on your part to store and distribute the content. If your reader orders your book at midnight on a Tuesday in Alabama and you are traveling in Europe for a few weeks, you do not have to figure out how to ship it to them—you can automate a message that sends the password to the gated content on your blog, and "poof!" they have instant access to your eBook right then. And for you, you do not have to worry about the added cost of all the physical products. Even though you can automate and sell digital products easily, you still have to worry about customer service and monitor sales though.

There are many advantages to selling digital "information products". Below are some of the major reasons to consider using this strategy to make money through your blog:

> 1. *Digital products are pretty easy to develop and are simple to design.* They are also inexpensive or even free to create. You may invest a little money into editing or adding a graphic design element to your products, but it is possible to come up with something valuable and amazing without spending anything more than your mental energy and time to

develop. The great added benefit with this is that, if the product does not sell like hotcakes, you are not out very much. This low risk is a great selling point for digital products.

2. *You do not have to pay for storage.* You can create it and store it on the Cloud, on your computer, and gated on your blog. No worry about inventory, inventory management, and storage for this method! And the illusion that you can just store physical inventory at your home is unrealistic and becomes very overwhelming and also limiting. Digital products do not require physical space, so take advantage!

So now that you know the value of offering these types of products through your blog, how do you create your valuable and relevant products? To start, you always want to begin with research. Determine what products are already selling for your niche. Your research can include visiting places like Amazon, eBay, online discussion boards, groups on social media, and major news sites. For digital products, make sure also to check Clickbank.com because they are focused primarily on digital products. It does offer information in other areas, but that is their primary niche. And once you get a good idea of what is and is not out there for your competition, you can also gather information about pricing as well. Keep in mind that you are not trying to be a pioneer here; you are looking to nudge your way into an already booming or blossoming trend for your niche. Being a pioneer is risky and often has more downsides to good. Instead, find a unique and personal voice to get into an already successful strategy. This means that there are a market and audience for this already—you just need to make sure that they see the value in what you have to offer.

Once you have an idea of what you want to offer and the price you want to charge for it, it is time to get down to actually creating it. For documents, develop them in Microsoft Word first and then save it as a PDF once you are done editing it. Make sure to get a professionally-designed cover for your document content. For example, hire a freelancer through Fiverr.com to come up with something nice to add to it. This can cost as little as $5, depending on the designer you choose and what your budget is. Even making a video can be little to no cost for you. Use your camera on your phone or point-and-shoot camera and then upload the video onto your computer. Use iMovie or Movie Maker, free software for most computer operating systems, to edit and refine the content. You can even add a nice audio file to it, making it look and sound more professional.

Creating an audio file is another interesting option for digital content. Just record your content through GarageBand or Sound Recorder and edit it when you are done. Make sure you have a good microphone for this type of content. For book writing, you do not need to be an expert in the written word to offer something informative and valuable to your readers. If you struggle with writing a book, consider hiring someone to do it for you. You can also interview professionals and record the interviews as a product. Another idea is to find digital products that are for sale and then rebrand the item to make it your own. There are many ways you can develop creative digital content and use it to make money, and you do not need to be an expert in creating this content format to be successful.

Once you get it created, you need to get it to your readers. Direct-response online marketing is a good way to push it out to millions of viewers, but it is not the most strategic or cost-effective. If you have the means to launch a big marketing push like this, give it a try. Otherwise, use your email mailing list to your advantage. Come up with a good and enticing email message and subject line to get your readers interested. From there, they can engage with your content, both free and paid for. The more you can mix free with paid information, the more you can generate interest and loyalty. Like traditional direct marketing campaigns, your email strategy will only result in a small number of people taking advantage of your digital products, but those small buyers should be bringing in a bit of profit.

And once those people buy something from you, you can target them again in the future to buy more things like it. You can follow up the initial purchase with another option that offers more value at a higher price. Doing this "back end" selling is a great way to boost the sales you already have from the "front end", and often lower priced, products. For example, you can bring in people with a short white paper on a topic and then follow up that sale with an offer to buy an eBook that goes into more detail on the same or similar topic. Or you can offer a short how-to guide for the front-end sale and then access to a training video as a follow-up, back-end sale. In addition to your direct, email marketing strategy, make sure to write a blog post that leads to the promotion of your product and shares the information on social media.

4. Selling digital services (webinars, courses, memberships, coaching, etc.)

Services that you offer through your blog are anything that does not have a physical presence like a product. Services are unique to your niche and your voice. This is one of the best reasons to offer a service to your readers; you can offer something no one else can, and in a way no one can replicate. Sometimes, you can figure out what you will offer as a service through the comments and questions by your readers. If there is a common theme or problem your readers continue to struggle with, how can you help them through consultations, meetings, coaching, etc.? In addition to offering them the information they are seeking, a service can also give them the feeling of personalized attention. A blog post can offer general advice, but a coaching session can cut right to what they need or want. Below are a few ideas for services you can offer:

- *Blogging advice or assistance.* You are already a blogger, so when a business wants to start blogging, you are someone worth listening to and learning from. Most likely, you have done a lot of research (like reading this book!) and have learned from a few mistakes. Bringing this experience to a client can be incredibly valuable.

- *Social media service.* Like the blogging service listed above, you are already using social media to your profit and advantage for your blog. Your experience with growing your followers, increasing engagement, and building traffic can be used to help others. This is especially helpful for small business owners. Offer your expertise for a fee that slides based on how much help they need.

Of course, there are many other innovative service ideas you can develop that are more directly related to your blog content, and a few will be covered more in depth in other sections such as webinars and memberships. No matter what you decide to offer, always make sure it benefits your readers the most. If you offer something that is low cost but highly valuable, you can have more sales and increase your reputation, benefiting you for the long term.

Once you settle on the service you want to offer, you have to consider a few important things, such as how much time it is going to take to fulfill your offer and how you plan on gathering payment for your services. Your services are just one way for you to make money through your blog. This means that you still need to have time to dedicate to other activities, like writing for your blog! Make sure you have a set amount of time set aside for your services, and you do not thin yourself out in the process. Understanding how much you want to make from your services and how many hours you can invest in the process each month can also help you define how much you want to charge. For example, if you want to make $1,500 per month through online mentoring, and you want to give about 30 hours per month to this service, you need to charge about $50 per hour for the service. This breaks out to about seven or eight hours per week dedicated to mentoring clients. Now, look at the average cost of this service for competition in your niche and the reality of dedicating eight hours in the week to mentoring. If both are realistic, you are in a good spot.

In addition to understanding the amount of time you have to dedicate to your services and your income goals, you can figure out just how much you are going to make from your services. Ideally, the need is far greater than your availability, and you can start booking up spaces, filling future spots, ensuring revenue in the future and helping establish your reputation as a leader in the market. Make sure to have a place on your blog to highlight your services and talk about what you are offering. Make sure to show your readers why it is valuable to work with you or use your services. You should also include the cost of your services on this page. Promote this content through email mailings, social media, in posts, etc. Then make it really easy for people to pay you. Keep it simple and straightforward. Offer a "shopping cart" and accept PayPal. PayPal also offers a plug-in for most blog platforms and hosting sites that you can take advantage of.

Coaching

This is like mentoring. It means working with someone, typically one on one, to help them achieve a goal. You can also offer a group coaching session with a small group of people working towards the same goal. You can conduct these sessions over an online video calling service, like Skype, or you can communicate just through email or phone. It is wise to record the sessions for follow-up and additional coaching support. Sometimes, you can even edit this content to create additional products to sell on your blog! Just make sure that your coaching client gets a copy of the recording with tips from you that are valuable and "homework" they need to complete before the next session.

People seek coaches to get them to grow and bound forward in a certain area. Typically, the people searching for a coach are new to a certain thing or field. If you have been in or know a lot about a certain topic, most likely connected to the content of your blog, you can be a host of information for them. In addition, you can charge a high amount for your hourly services! One very important thing to keep in mind is that you need to make sure you are the right coach for the client. If your client is looking for answers that are more in depth or out of your range, do not try to fake it just to get their money. Let them know you are not the best fit for them and try to help them find someone else to help them. You will not only save your reputation, but you will also create a thankful, and possibly loyal, follower after that honest transaction.

Memberships

You have much to offer your readers. You are personal, sharing, and helpful. If your readers want more from you, offer it to them for a monthly fee. For example, readers who want more access to things you have to offer, consider signing them up for a gym-like membership to a special part of your blog. When they have a membership, offer them access to things like software, apps, templates, checklists, worksheets, recorded or live webinars, videos, how-to documents, reports, articles, etc. There are many reasons people choose to join a membership, but the main reasons are to make their life more simple or easy, to help them learn something faster, or get more details on information found online.

You should consider developing a membership site because of the many opportunities it offers you. One of the biggest ones is the steady income it offers. You know that you can count on their monthly membership fee each month as part of your revenue. If you are offering them valuable content that is refreshed often, you will retain your members month after month. Having a membership also helps boost your reputation as a leader in your niche. And the more your reputation spreads as a leader and expert, the more people that will sign up for your membership! It is a great spiral of success. In addition, it opens up more doors for selling services and products, like eBooks and coaching services. As you make your members happy with great content, you can count on them telling their friends, family, and co-workers about it too. This brings in more clients and readers, and these referrals are often the best leads for your business. If you want to encourage this type of word of mouth referral, consider offering an affiliate program to your members with a benefit to them for their referral that joins the membership program.

It may sound like a large time commitment and a lot of work to come up with a valuable membership site. Yes, it will take time from your week to make it great, but you can automate many things. Once you create content, you can create a strategy to engage your members without having to do a lot of new development or interaction. This then turns your membership into a very passive form of income that you can almost set it and forget it. After all, your membership site is online, so you can work on it or adjust things as needed from any place and at any time. All you need is a device with access to the Internet.

The challenge with running a membership site is that you do need to keep it fresh. Your clients need to have access to relevant and timely information in relation to your niche. And you almost always need to be recruiting members to your membership group so you can replace those that leave (some will leave no matter what you do or do not do. There are things outside of your control that influence people to quit memberships or cancel services) and build your income stream and reputation. In addition, while you can run a membership through email, most of the successful options offer them online. This means you will probably need to pay a bit more for these types of tools for your blog to function properly. And while it is possible to offer a quality membership as an automated service, you will still need to offer fresh content often. If you are charging a monthly fee for access to your most valuable information, make sure it is fresh often. In addition, consider offering a monthly webinar for members to discuss a certain topic in more detail, offer a free half hour of coaching, or give them early access to tools or tips that you have not yet released to the public.

Depending on your niche, your membership site may look different than others. For example, some membership sites are only for courses and webinar training. This is great for a niche that is technical or very complex. Another example of a membership site is one that offers reports, papers, and articles that are premium for the niche. Think of academic and scientific journals. These sites are memberships and require members to pay to access the entire content in their library. Another idea is to create a special community place to share ideas or discuss topics with like-minds, or a place to share trending news in a specific field. You can also offer digital content through your membership site instead of selling it individually. For example, if you have a lot of graphics, instead of selling rights to each one, you can have a membership set up so a client can access all your content for a set fee each month.

Honestly, just about any type of niche and any type of blogger can benefit from having a membership site as part of their blog. Even for hobbyists, creating a place for people to come and discuss topics or access information is invaluable in helping continue to offer value for the future. Memberships are valuable and can help in numerous ways. Think of what your niche and readers are already interested in, and figure out what you can do to make a membership beneficial to their life. Also, make sure you create the content for your membership site before you build and promote it. You want to give a great experience to your first few members, so spend time coming up with quality content for them, just like you would do if you have 1,000 members.

Once you launch your membership site, make sure it is active. Keep your content fresh and relevant. Work on recruiting new members often. Encourage a sense of community and a place for members to interact with one another. This is also a great place for you to engage with them. Reply to comments and questions promptly and be prepared to get more detailed, personal, or informative in these discussions than you would in a typical blog post. Your readers are paying for more of you, so make sure to give it to them here.

Webinars

Webinars are an amazing service you can give to your readers. You can offer live webinars or record content and sell it to them for anytime access. The purpose of the webinar is to bring resources and tips on a specific topic to one place. Then it is synthesized into a lesson format and presented to clients to help solve their problem or teach them something important to them. The information shared needs to be practical, useful, and applicable. The people who pay for your webinar should walk away with a new skill they can put into action. In addition to sharing knowledge, webinars are a great place to also promote your blog and other services or products for sale. Some of the best ways to make money through your webinars are by:

- *Dig into the topic and find as much relevant information as possible.* Keep it handy while presenting your information, even if you do not use all of it in the presentation. It is possible that you will get a question about it or that you will find it useful to interject additional content as you are presenting. This also shows your clients that you are an expert, know your stuff, and are well prepared. You show them that this presentation matters to you. The more fully developed and well prepared and edited your webinar is, the more success and profits you can expect.

- *Select your software carefully.* When you are preparing to host a webinar, you need to find a software program that makes sense for you and is good for your clients as well. In addition, you can choose a free option, or you can upgrade your webinar for a fee. Stick to your budget and what makes the most sense for your clients and yourself. ezTalks Webinar is an easy resource that does not cost a lot. It also is known for offering tools helpful in presenting a webinar in a user-friendly manner. Some of these helpful tools include whiteboard sharing, recording, surveys, polls, and reporting.

- *Share content on your webinar well.* If you are referring to links or other sites often throughout your presentation, offer those resources to your clients. You could even send the list of resources being discussed to them before the actual event so that they can read ahead of time, but it also can instill a sense of confidence in their choice to pay for your webinar because you have clearly done a lot of research into what you are presenting to them. Another option is to sell your resource list as an add-on to your webinar. If you can give them access to a lot of additional content on the topic, they are likely willing to follow up your discussion with those resources you recommend and sell to them.

- *Promote outside and within.* Promote your webinar to the public through all the channels you can, including writing a blog teaser about it. And once you are presenting your webinar, include information and links to your other products, services, and blog. You can even offer a webinar to walk through another product you are selling. This way, if you sell the client that product, you can then follow up the sale with the webinar to help them get the most out of their purchase. Then your webinar can focus on some of the more nuanced features of your product and how they can get the most from it. This format further allows clients to talk with you in real time about their purchase and you can get fresh feedback that you can follow up on and ask more questions about, so you can better tailor your content and offerings for your readers and clients.

5. Selling physical products (Inventory and Dropshipping)

You do not need to just offer your readers access to digital content for solving their problems and answering their questions. You can come up with a physical product to offer them. You can create something one-of-a-kind and sell it or purchase a bit of inventory and offer it for sale. If you do not have the time, money or space to hold on to inventory, another option for selling physical inventory is dropshipping. Basically, this is when you list items for sale on your website but do not hold the inventory yourself. The manufacturer or another third-party seller holds on to the inventory until your reader places an order. Once they place an order with you, you turn around and place the order with the third-party. They are the ones that gather the product, package it, and ship it to your customer.

There are two ways you can determine pricing for dropshipped products. First, base your pricing on the quality and value of the item. If a product is more valuable to your readers, price it higher. Or, if you have two products for sale, price the lower quality one lower, and increase the price for the one of better quality. The second approach is determining the price based on what it costs you to sell it. For example, if you know that the sale of a certain item is going to cost you about $10, your price better is higher than $10. You can typically get drop shipped items at wholesale or very inexpensive, leaving a lot of room for profit.

It is not all easy and glorious, though. You do give up a lot of control by doing this. You cannot control who or when your supplier processes the order and ships the item to the customer. In addition, you cannot typically add your own branding materials to the package as a traditional retailer could. Also, quality could be unknown if you do not first purchase a test item from the supplier so you could be sending poor items to your customers, leading to negative reviews and increased customer service needs. You must decide if the products you want to offer to your readers are worth the sacrifices.

To add drop shipping to your blog, look for plug-ins like jigoshop, ecwild, or woocommerce. Another popular option is the AliDropship plug-in. Other platforms offer e-commerce such as shopify and oberlo. Before you get too far into this, check with your blog platform to see if they offer an e-commerce function already that you can use or see if they are optimized for one of these plug-ins. Keep in mind that the focus is on your blog and then on products, so do not get too caught up in making sure your blog can sell these products from it. You can always find a workaround if you cannot.

Chapter 5: Managing Your Multiple Passive Income Streams

Your Blog: Your New Business Platform

In order for you to have long-term success with your profitable blog, you need to think a bit like a businessperson. Again, as mentioned much earlier in this book, blogging is not a passive income stream. You can make passive income through your blog, but the act of blogging and building a successful blog is often a full-time job. It requires constant content creation, networking, and marketing. Most of the time, the biggest hurdle to your success is your perceptions. You may have come to blogging with the illusion that you will be raking in piles of money while hardly lifting a finger. Paid advertisements would grace the edges of a beautiful site while sponsors are begging you to try their products and offering large sums of cash to talk about them. This is not always the case, and when this does not happen, you may slip into the mindset that blogging, therefore, cannot make you money like "promised". This is not the best method of approaching your blogging business, because, after all, it is a business to make you income. It is time to make sure your mind is thinking like a business.

For starters, you came to blogging because you have a voice and you want to use that voice to talk about a certain niche. This may create the illusion that you can talk about whatever you want whenever you want because this is your platform to do so. This is a Hobbyist perspective. You are here to make money and share your opinion. This means you need to approach as more like an Entrepreneur. Like any good business, you need a plan for success. You need to think of strategy and growth. It needs to stop being about you and your whims and more about those that you want to reach. Yes, this can be complicated and hard. It takes time and attention, and often a learning curve. However, you came to blogging to write, not fret about data analytics! Well, if you are coming to blogging also to create an income, you need to delve a bit into this as well. The business of running a business is not that complicated. You need to simply offer a solution to the problem your niche is facing. If you can find a big enough problem, and can clearly share your solution to people, you are going to succeed. It is all the little details that can feel like the whole thing is bogging you down. If you ever feel like this, pull yourself back to this basic understanding and come at it again from a fresh approach. You will do great with this perspective.

It can also be hard to justify to yourself and others why you are spending money on a blog. It is especially hard to justify when the blog is not making you any money yet. Expecting a business to boom overnight is unrealistic. Sure, it has happened a time or two to a select few, but for the majority of business owners, it took years for their investment in their business to pay off. Blogging is a business if you want it to make you money. This means you need to "spend money to make money." No, you do not want to go spending thousands on random paid advertisements without training or strategy, but you do want to spend money on getting the skills and best tools in place to set up your opportunity for success.

A great advantage of online business like a blog is that you are not tied to a physical location, but sometimes, bloggers act like they are. They act like their audience has to come to their blog to read their content, and therefore, make money. The reality is: you can go to your readers too. You do not always have to make them come back to your website in order to have a successful blog. You can share the content straight through an email or valuable information only on Facebook. The idea is to establish yourself as a value giver. This is what creates loyalty and a strong following. This is what leads to long-term success and good revenue streams. You are not tied to your blog, waiting and wishing for someone to engage with it. Get it out there and mingle with the digital world!

If you sat holed up in your house all day you would also lose touch with what your friends, family, and clients are doing. You would not know what they really needed from you. You may even wonder what you could possibly offer them to help fulfill their needs. You need to get out and engage so that you can get an idea of what is really happening in your niche. You can also find pockets of people that have not heard your voice and solution yet. You have no geographic or other boundaries that traditional businesses struggle with, so take advantage of it. There is so much opportunity.

All this opportunity and business can feel exhausting. And in the beginning, it is hard, but as you get used to the process and work your plan, you will find a rhythm that is sustainable for you. In addition, you will probably and should be developing a network of other bloggers to help support and grow your blog. And in return, you should be helping and supporting theirs. Of course, you will want to choose your blogger network carefully, making sure it is a quality connection that encourages this growth mindset. Do not jump on the "hamster wheel" of meaningless comments and empty "views" just for the sake of fluffing up numbers. Look for content, quality, and value even in these connections, and you will create a sustainable and long-term blog that you are both proud of and profiting from. Change your mindset to that of a businessperson, and you can grow your blog-business effectively.

Not Just a Side-Hustle: Go Full-Time on Passive Income

Throughout this book, you have been exposed to tools, tips, and techniques for creating and running a successful, money-making blog. However, now that you know all of this information, it is time to set it in motion and make it happen. To begin, you need an objective. This is a description of how you will begin shifting your focus full time onto your blog while creating full-time income (hopefully!).

Here are some tips on how to help you get clear on what you want so you can move from "side hustle" to "full time":

1. *Get clear on what you want to do.* You will learn more about how to set a realistic and attainable goal in the next section of this chapter, but you should have an idea of the goal, even if the goal at this point is just to turn your "side hustle" into "full time". Keep this goal in mind as you go forward, so you stay on the path where you intend to go.

2. *Slow growth is still growth.* In fact, slow is good. Just because you made a little bit of money through your blog does not mean you are ready to let your full-time job go just yet. Instead, move slow, and make sure your blog is a sustainable income source. The first few months of juggling basically two full-time jobs is tough and exhausting. This is where a plan comes in handy, but recognize that this is not forever and you will have a break soon. Just keep plugging along as best you can until you can make the transition.

3. *Make friends and connections.* You need to get your name out there. You need to be noticed. This can be uncomfortable, but remember that this is for your business. This is not you personally posting about your dog, but rather sharing it to grow your income and support your life. In fact, starting out, be bold and tell people you are connected to on social media what you are working on and ask them for help! Get them on your side and invested in your success too! Just by putting it out there and being honest can grow your business by leaps and bounds.

4. *Pump up your followers in all areas.* Yes, you are writing a blog. But if you learned nothing from the previous chapters about social media, you need to use it to your advantage. This means getting more and more people to follow you in different places so that you can lead them back time and time again to your blog posts. You do not need to shy away from asking them to follow you from one place to the other. Ask your Facebook friends to follow you on Pinterest and Instagram. When you move from a side gig to full-time hustle, you want to have some hype around it. Having a strong social presence is a great way to boost that news the minute you go big.

5. *Let the fear help you fly as you leap into a full-time blogger status.* You will be scared at some point. Fear will play a big or small role in your transition, but it will be there. You will also have self-doubt—if not others doubting you. You will probably think that stalling before you go full time is good. After all, the second tip on this list is to move slow. However, at some point, you will know you are ready to leap into this but are afraid to do it. To make sure you are ready, make sure to check off the following:

> a. You have set a clear and realistic plan to turn your side hustle blog into a full-time income.
>
> b. You are already making good money from your blog.
>
> c. Your blog and income are growing steadily over time.
>
> d. Your instincts are telling you that it is time, even if your head is telling you a "rational" reason not to.

What Next?

Now that you have these introductory tips and advice, you are ready to get going and give it a try! All this information can feel overwhelming (see comments on this in the first part of this chapter!), so the following are a few time management tips to help you get started with it all. Sometimes, it helps to look at a calendar for the rest of the year, imagine where you want to be by December, and start planning a posting strategy to get you there. Your goal can be financial or traffic-related or simply to be consistently blogging from now until then. Consistency is vital to your success, so focusing on this, especially in the beginning, can help keep you on track and motivated.

There is so much information on this topic, and always something more to learn as the online landscape continues to change and evolve. While you get started, remain a student of the process. Learn and read as much as you can to help you grow. The tips in this book are relevant to helping you get started right now, but in the future, new advancements, options, opportunities, and changes may shift the advice here and your approach out there. The important thing is that you get going and give it a try. Insert different strategies to bring in passive income through your blog, keep a finger on the pulse of your niche, and allow your personality and voice to ring strong in all the valuable content you produce.

Below are some tips to help you manage your time starting your profitable blog:

- Determine the goal for your blog and keep that goal posted where you can see it. Make sure you set "S.M.A.R.T." goals. This means goals that are "specific, measurable, attainable, relevant, and timely." An example of a "S.M.A.R.T." goal is below. The blank lines under the example are for you to try your hand at writing your own "S.M.A.R.T." goal:
    - o Specific: Increase page views by 15%
    - o Specific: _____
    _____

    - o Measurable: Using Google Analytics to watch the fluctuations in views from current until reaching a 15% increase.

o Measurable: _____

_____
_____

o Attainable: Page views will grow through an increased focus on lead generation, which includes a more aggressive posting schedule, guest blog strategy, and a challenge.

o Attainable: _____

_____
_____
_____
_____
_____

o Relevant: Increasing page views will elevate my blog's ability to get sponsorships and more income through affiliate links.

o Relevant: _____

_____
_____

o Timely: The increase will occur over the next nine months in response to the activities planned for that time frame.

o Timely: _____

_____

- Plan ahead for how you will succeed. This means looking at all the actions you need to do in a day and week and setting a specific amount of time to do it. Do not "hope" to fit it into your day at some point. Instead, carve out hours to dedicate to your blog's success. Consider the following actions and what days and times you will give to these activities:

o Research: _____

_____

o Writing: _____

_____

o Editing: _____

_____

o Comment response: _____

_____

o Promotion: _____

_____

o Review other blogs: _____

_____

o Comment on other blogs: _____

_____

- Keep a notebook on you at all times to track your ideas. This can be an electronic method for taking notes, or it can be a physical journal you carry around. Whatever you decide, just make sure you have a way to write down the brilliant thoughts that pop into your head or the cool observations you make throughout the day. This is especially helpful if blogging is not your full-time job. Setting time aside to brainstorm can be a challenge. You can also snap a picture of something interesting you see while out or ask to record an engaging conversation.

- Friends are the best people to start with when it comes to research. This means going to coffee with a few friends, or giving them a quick call, and asking their opinion about what you are researching. Write down their impressions of the topic. This can also help you redefine how you present the concept. For example, if you pose a question to them and they get confused about what you are asking, work out how to rephrase it, so they get it, and then use that rephrase to help in writing your content. Once you get their perspective, then add in some information you find online to round out the fresh approach.

- When you set time for work, do nothing but work. This means getting rid of anything can distract you. Turn off the TV, silence your phone, turn off notifications online, etc. The time you set for this is important and deserves your attention. Give it all you got for the time you set for it, and then get up and go back to handling life. The chances are that your world will not fall apart for an hour or two while you get work done. (Of course, if it is an emergency and the world is falling apart, go handle it and then reschedule the time for your blog later in the day or that week.)

- As you sit down to write your first blog post or your 400th, you need to approach it the same way: write. Do not worry about the editing bit that is scheduled for later. It is scheduled for a reason. This time you have for writing is meant for just that; writing. Do not fret over the introductory sentence or the flow from one paragraph to another. If staring at a blank page is intimidating, consider developing an outline and flushing it out from there. This helps to keep your points on target. While you are flowing, you will probably come up with just the right sentence to start or intro into the topic.

- Do not try to be everything to everyone, including to you. If you are terrible at editing photos or do not understand Photoshop, outsource it. If you are struggling with keeping up with your email blasts and editing, hire someone. You can get a virtual assistant that can take on a lot of the day-to-day tasks, or you can purchase quality images and video for a low price on sites like fiverr.com, elance.com, and freelancer.com. You only have 24 hours in a day, and there are many commitments you need to handle during that time. If you find you are struggling with getting it all done, look for ways to get help. It may cost you more than you like in the beginning, but when you are bringing in a good stream of income from your blog, it will be worth it.

- Use the automation and scheduler tools available. You can schedule just about everything from your social media posts to publishing a new blog. Consider scheduling assistants like Buffer, Everypost, and Hootsuite to help you. With a service like this, you no longer have to log into each social site individually to develop your posts, but just plan it out in one place, tell it when to make it public, and move on. If budget is your concern, try out TweetDeck for your Facebook and Twitter accounts, but be aware that it is limited.

- If you are struggling with coming up with fresh content still, reach out for a guest blog or reader perspectives on a topic. Maybe even once a week, offer a chance for your readers to be heard or other bloggers to chime in with their thoughts. This is an amazing way to engage your readers, connect other bloggers and their audience to your site, and strengthen your reputation in your niche.

- Read and follow other bloggers that are your direct and indirect competition. Yes, part of your job is to read interesting blogs! You are not doing this to copy and plagiarize what others are doing, but what you are doing is getting ideas of what is already being talked about and how it is presented and what is still left on the table about a certain topic. You can also refine your voice in your writing by seeing how others present their ideas to their audience. In addition, it allows you to connect with other bloggers in your niche and create meaningful partnerships and discussions that benefit you both.

Conclusion

Thank you for making it through to the end of *Blogging For Beginners: Proven Strategies for Marketing Your Blog in 2020 and Making a Profit with Your Writing by Creating Multiple Streams of Passive Income.* It should have been informative and provided you with all of the tools you need to achieve your goals, whatever they may be.

Now that you have learned about the basics, you are ready to start developing content, getting onto your blog, and making some money. Use the tools in this guide to choose the best platform and topics for your posts. Decide how you are going to generate income, possibly through a mix of affiliate links and digital content or e-commerce. Schedule your posts to go live and set up a social media marketing strategy to promote your content. Work on your strategy to develop your mailing list and lead generation, so you continue to bring people to your blog and begin establishing yourself as an expert in your niche.

Blogging takes a bit of time to establish yourself in your field, so put in the effort with the understanding that it will pay off in the long run as long as you stick to it. Remember why you are doing it by keeping your goal posted where you can see it often. And always keep your focus on your readers, not on yourself. Bring your passion to them, and it will not only benefit both parties, but you will be more successful for longer this way. The more you benefit your readers, the more you will make. It may sound simple, but it is easy to forget. If you find yourself slipping away from being customer focused, put up another note posted by the goal that brings you back to them. You will not regret it!

And if you find yourself continuing to slip, question, or wonder, remember you can always come back to this resource to help you build and grow. Of course, this is designed for the beginner in mind, but these foundational concepts are always good to reflect on as you grow. Sometimes, simple is the best! You are on the precipice of living a life of passion and purpose, being paid to contribute your voice to the world. Now is the time to spring forward, grab your future, and enjoy your success. You have the drive, the tools, and passion. Now all you need is the action! You are ready!

Finally, if you found this book useful in any way, a review on Amazon is always appreciated!

Part 2: Blogging

Unlock the Secrets to Making Your Blog Posts into Profit and Discover How Bloggers Make Money Online Utilizing Affiliate Marketing and Other E-Commerce Skills for Passive Income

Introduction

The following chapters will discuss the best secrets and strategies for becoming a pro-blogger and creating passive income. Making money online isn't something that only a select few special individuals get to do. You can do it too, as long as you have the drive and the information to do so.

The first stop along our journey will be looking at how people can blog for profit. The most important thing to figure out is if you are already a pro-blogger. Now, if you don't already have a blog, that's okay. In fact, it might be easier for you to become a pro-blogger because you are starting fresh. That doesn't mean, however, that you can't take an already formed blog and revamp it to make it profitable.

Then, we will move into the first blogging secret, which is content marketing. This means we will look at picking a niche, creating the best content, email marketing, and effective strategies. This is where everybody will have to start.

Then, we'll move into the second secret, which is affiliate marketing. This is the first way bloggers make money. Picking affiliate marketing networks can be hard to do, but we'll discuss how to pick the best, and how to be a market affiliate with Amazon.

Then, secret number three will discuss e-commerce and dropshipping. This is the second way you can make money with your blog. Selling products no longer means you have to have actual products on hand. Dropshipping has changed the game, and we will discuss the best way to use it.

Then, onto secret number four: expert information products. Much like the last secret, you will be selling a product, but this time it will be your expertise. This could mean writing a book, creating courses, or webinars.

Then, we will look at the last secret: advertising. This is a biggie, and something most people struggle with. It can be confusing to figure out how to advertise your blog or products, but it doesn't have to be. We will look at the best way to drive traffic to your site and to become a ninja at Google AdSense.

Chapter 1: Pro Blogging for Profit: How It's Really Done

You might not be new to the blogging game, but did you know that you can turn your blog into money? If you have thought about turning your blog into a professional blog, it could be the best decision you will ever make. You may not have even thought about professional blogging, but if you are brave enough to take a leap, it might make a new life for you. Don't get me wrong, being a professional blogger isn't easy. It takes time, knowledge, and skills to turn a blog into an income-generating, full-time job. Read on to find out more.

Are You a Pro Blogger?

Before you take that leap of faith, you have to understand that many things have changed over the past few years with blogging. Blogging isn't an easy and simple way to create income. But blogging is a very reputable way to make money online. If you commit to learning how to do it right and work hard, you can earn up to $1,000 a month with your blog.

You have to remember that when you want to make money by blogging, you have to approach and treat it just like a real business. Many bloggers have jumped into the river of professional blogging, however during the 2011 and 2012 Google Penguin and Google Panda updates, many blogs drowned. These bloggers decided to turn to other types of online marketing.

The reality is: if you don't stick with it, you are going to fail.

When making the decision to be a professional blogger full time, you have to consider many things, like your financial and social situation.

If you are single and don't have any family responsibilities, you might be able to handle all the risks. If you already have a full-time job that provides your family with security, you should first talk it over with everyone involved to see if taking that risk is worth it.

When you first start out blogging professionally, you need to figure out how many hours you can put into it. If you only have about three or four hours a day to commit to your blog, you might make about $400 to $500 a month. If you can work twelve to sixteen hours each day, you could increase your income drastically. If you have a family life, those hours might be too much for you to do.

Your income is going to come from sources like affiliate marketing, Google AdSense, direct ads, and other services. In order to be a successful professional blogger making a reliable income, you need to have certain skills.

You need to have professional skills in:

- Management.

- Email marketing.

- Social media marketing.

- Search engine optimization (SEO).

- Writing.

If you already have a blog, you might have some of these skills. If you can acquire any new skills that you don't currently have, and successfully implement them, then you can learn to be a professional blogger.

You have to be different from every blogger out there. You have to be unique. You have to be special. You have to be better than everybody else in your field.

To be able to do this, you have to strengthen your weaknesses:

- If you can't figure out what is wrong, ask for feedback.

- If your blog is boring, find ways to engage with others more.

- If your writing isn't that great, practice your writing.

1. Figure Out What You Want

If you want peace of mind when you are transitioning into professional blogging, the first thing you need to do is to figure out ways to make a recurring fixed income with your blog. When you are positive that you can survive comfortably from your blog, only then should you even think about quitting your job to be a full-time blogger.

Before you take this important step, make sure to write out a business plan and road map. You need to think about these things:

- Are you willing to learn new things?

- Are there ways to expand your blog?

- Are there ways you can bring attention to your blog?

- How will you brand your blog?

- What sources of income are you going to use?

- What will your marketing strategy look like?

- Where will you get your traffic?

You have to take the time to think about and develop your blog. What do you want it to be like? This is a very important stage for you, to grow your blog and for you to identify avenues to develop it in the future.

2. Being a Professional Blogger

It could take you anywhere from six months to a number of years to make the decision to become a professional blogger. The blogging world has gotten larger over the past few years. You need to be well equipped to rely on blogging as your full-time income.

Keep in mind the old quote: "Never put all your eggs in one basket."

Even though the blogging world is volatile, when you are trying to become a professional blogger, you have to protect yourself in every way possible. If you only have one blog that is making you money, you need to try to expand your empire so that a catastrophic problem doesn't bankrupt you.

If you have a good blog, you might begin making a decent amount of money in about four to five months.

3. College Students

If you are a college student, you need to start a blog. Being in college allows you to have many social engagements, freedom, and endless opportunities to get your life ready for success. If you can publish a blog with ten articles each month, by the end of your first year you will have published 120 articles. By the time you graduate from college, you will have a well-aged blog with about 500 articles.

Passive Income: Your Game Changer

Let's begin by finding out what passive income actually is: passive income is money that you earn in ways that don't take a lot of effort. Some types of passive income include renting out property that you own, or blogging. It might take some time and effort to get these revenue streams started, but then you can make money while you are sleeping.

To many people, blogging is just a hobby. If you want to make lots of money, you need to look at it as a business. Some bloggers are going to struggle to make enough money to cover the expenses of running their blog, like their electric and internet bills. Other bloggers have pulled in over one million dollars each year. While nothing is ever guaranteed, I can tell you that if you are diligent, your rewards could be tremendous.

How much money you make all depends on the traffic your site gets. You can make between one and ten cents per page view. This means that if you generate about 50,000 views each month, you will be making between $500 and $5,000 each month.

There aren't any definitive sources on the amount of money you could make blogging, but one survey done by a website called ProBlogger surveyed 1,500 bloggers and found the following:

- Four percent brought in a five-figure salary each month.
- Thirteen percent made above $1,000 each month.
- Fifty-three percent made less than $100 each month.
- Ten percent didn't make anything.

4. How to Make Money

You can make money with your blog and with opportunities that might show up because you have a site. Here are some methods:

1. Services.

Blogging creates credibility and could help make you seem like an expert on a certain subject. This will give you an opportunity to maneuver into services that pay, like:

- Investments.
- Performing specific services like social media marketing, fixing websites, or creating websites.
- Speaking.
- Coaching.

2. Selling products.

To do this you just have to use your blog's content to make readers want to purchase a product from your site. These can be separated into digital and physical products:

- Digital.
- Memberships.
- Exclusive access through your site.

- Premium content.

- Online courses.

- E-books.

- Physical.

- Retail items like jewelry, clothing, etc.

- Books.

3. Affiliate marketing.

With this type of marketing, you are going to recommend services or products on your website. You, in turn, will make a commission or percentage of all sales. Companies know you have readers that are loyal and trust you. They will check out other businesses because you recommended them. This doesn't cost your readers anything.

This is a money-making strategy that is powerful for blogs that have a certain niche. If you write about photography and you think that a certain course might be a good fit for your audience, you put a link to this course on your blog and for every signup that happens by clicking on this link, you will get a commission. You could also recommend a product they can purchase from Amazon, then you get paid if somebody purchases something through your site.

You can create your relationships with companies that work with your niche or you can use a company such as Flex Offers or Commission Junction.

Affiliate marketing has the potential to be a great deal for everybody, since businesses are getting introduced to audiences, readers are finding out about services or products, and you get a commission from connecting the two.

4. Advertising.

Advertisers are looking for ways to get exposed and to find new customers. If you give them a place to be seen, you could get money for it. This type of advertising comes in many forms:

- Sponsored Posts: This is a type of marketing that involves creating and sharing material like social media posts, blogs, and videos that don't promote a brand but want to create an interest in its services or products. Businesses want their products to be seen on various sites and know that through links it will help their ratings. They are usually willing to pay you between $50 and thousands of dollars to put their products or services on your blog.

- Brand Partnerships: Companies are willing to pay influencers. Blogging can be a great way to capitalize on this, but people who use Instagram usually do particularly well with it. Companies know that certain people have audiences that can be reached through association with them. All they want you to do is to refer, wear, or mention them on your blog or Instagram account.

- Display Advertising: You may have been on a site where you saw an ad on a sidebar or in the upper banner spot. You might see some in email posts or in newsletters.

- Contextual Ads: You will use a company such as Mediavine, Media.net, or Google AdSense. You are giving a space on your blog to a company that will fill that space with ads that your audience will see. You might have noticed that what you search for on Google follows you onto specific sites, where your searches suddenly show up as ads. This is a contextual ad. You could get paid for how many times the ad is clicked on or seen by visitors to your site. This is called either cost per click or cost per impression.

- Private/Direct Ads: You will work with the company to display their product. This is also called a banner or static ad.

The company will choose what they would like to show in a specific size box on your blog. You will set a price and they will pay you yearly, monthly, or daily to keep this on your blog.

5. Making It Successful

This part isn't all that easy. Anyone who has ever told you that you can just "Put some content up and begin bringing in the cash" is lying. It is going to take time to understand that running a blog is like running a business. You have to create your content and then build up trust and readers. Here are some steps you need to take:

• Create Your Blog: There have been many people who say they want to make money with their blog but they don't ever do this step. You need to begin somewhere.

• Find Content: You have to create content that will focus on specific niches that you are passionate about and that will draw in readers. You want a niche that is big enough for an audience but not so huge that you are going to get lost in the crowd.

• You Have to Stay Consistent: You have to be sure you are creating content consistently. This will help build a brand and people will want to see your content.

• Promoting Your Blog: It is wonderful for you to write an amazing blog, but what happens if nobody knows about it? You have to be active on social media. You have to network with other bloggers. Never be afraid of letting people know you are out there.

6. Will It Be Worth It?

This all depends on what you want out of it. You might not have any expectations as to the amount of money you can make blogging. I know I began my blog as a dare but it has turned into a lot more.

Most blogs will die before they are one year old. This is because, at first, you spend a lot of time writing without getting any money from it. It doesn't make sense when you look at it on paper, but if you can learn to be persistent, all the hard work will pay off with time. This sounds very much like passive income. You work hard at first then you get the payoff later.

You have to build a relationship with your readers, too. You can't measure that in money, but these readers are valuable in other ways.

Beginning a blog will allow you to be more flexible if you have a day job that you absolutely love and don't want to give up. You will be able to switch shifts, give up a shift or two, spend time with friends and family, and have more freedom overall.

If this sounds good to you, beginning a blog might be worth the time and effort.

$10,000+ a Month: Success Stories of Popular Bloggers

Blogging can be very profitable. I am sure you are wondering how in the world these bloggers can bring in loads of profits. Well, I have found the most successful bloggers who were willing to tell me their success stories and give us a sneak peek at what they do behind the scenes.

7. Neil Patel

Neil is an internet marketing guru who has earned over one million dollars a year with blogging. He is also a digital marketer who runs Hello Bar, QuickSprout, and Kissmetrics. He credits blogging with being his best revenue generator. He puts aside between five and six thousand dollars to help with his blog creations. He brings in over seven hundred thousand visitors in just one month. This turns into over 8,000 leads. These leads came solely from his blog. Here are some pointers from Neil:

- Your page subheadings and title only give you a few seconds to grab a person's attention. These sections count tremendously. You have to show your readers in the blink of an eye what they can expect when they read your blog.

- The length of your article doesn't matter as long as the point is clear and valuable. Don't forget the visual aids.

- Your blog needs to give your readers advice that is valuable, actionable, and clear.

- Network with other bloggers. Make sure you answer everybody's questions in a timely manner and make them actionable, helpful and detailed. Don't give them fluff.

- Add in an "opt-in" box at the end of all your blogs.

- Your content has to be exceptional to increase the traffic to your blog.

8. Pat Flynn

He has earned over two hundred thousand dollars in just one year. He went from being unemployed to being an internet sensation in a very short time. His blog called Smart Passive Income has made about two million dollars in revenue. Here are some of the things he did to accomplish this:

- Be a consultant. These services are something that can't be outsourced and are a great source of income. You have to create a good reputation and have quality learning materials so you can make your price large enough to be worthwhile.

- Online courses. Selling courses online is great since you only have to spend some money and time to make these. From there, you just resell them as long as they don't become obsolete.

- Create a podcast. Some people are visual learners, while others are auditory. Some people might just be too busy to read. Podcasts allow you to serve various audiences. If you do decide to create a podcast, add in a transcript.

- Make a membership site. This is a great source of stable and recurring income. Make sure your members get quality support and content.

- Write an e-book and publish it. Write about something you know well. You could also compile all your blogs into one book and sell these, too.

- Write about what you know and love. You can educate your readers with your blog posts.

9. Matthew Woodward

He is an internet marketing blogger who brings in over $20,000 each month. His success proves that anybody can make a living with blogging. He didn't use any links or SEO strategies. His entire blog is a case study about what happens if you only followed Google's Webmaster Guidelines without any SEO.

As of November 2017, he has earned well over one million dollars. His monthly revenue averages about $20,000. He earns his money from consultations, ads, and affiliate commissions. Here are some pointers from Matthew:

- Create competitions.

- Create video tutorials. Remember to post the transcript.

- Offer your readers exclusive content if they share or sign up. Be sure you offer them something they can't resist.

- When you set up your blog, you need to have an end goal in mind. It might be making money through affiliate commissions, selling products, subscribing to emails, social media, or a newsletter.

- You have to write the way you speak. You need to be straightforward and direct.

- Create a section of your blog for questions. This can be your topic for the next blog.

- Post your blog on forums like WarriorForum and TrafficPlanet. Interact with readers through their comments and always reply to their emails.

- Know what your audience wants and create your content from there.

10. Ramit Sethi

He created the I Will Teach You To Be Rich Blog. He earned five million dollars in just six days. He has over one million readers each month and has eight hundred thousand subscribers to his newsletter. Here is some advice he freely gives:

- Take an hour daily for some strategizing.

- Don't work with cheap clicks – they won't give you much revenue. Use quality products or services, deliver, and charge.

- If you have a customer who is interested in your product but you know it won't work for them, tell them and point them toward another product that will. Yes, you will be losing a sale but you will be gaining a person's trust.

- Whatever content you choose to write about, make sure 80 percent is valuable and leave the other 20 percent for your sales pitches.

- Know exactly what you want your ideal customer to be. Visualize your business as a high-end boutique where you only serve the best work, you can choose who you allow inside.

- Give away free material. After you have established that you are a quality provider, you can start charging big bucks for the products you sell.

- Don't spread yourself too thin. Focus on just a few great things at a time.

- If you don't want to be another fly by night business, don't conform to the standard. Follow your taste and find your vibe. People will soon be flocking to your products. Just don't try to reinvent the wheel with everything.

- Focus on finding 1,000 loyal customers who will stand by you and your products. This is better than having hundreds of thousands of readers who aren't interested at all.

11. Lena Gott

She is the founder and blogger of What Mommy Does. She earns more than $10,000 each month. Since she is a stay at home mom, she works anywhere between 20 and 25 hours weekly, which is hard to do with children. She makes her money from affiliate commissions, sponsored posts, e-books, and ads. Here are some pointers from her:

- Be useful and helpful. This is the best way to get your readers' trust.

- Add in other media. You don't have to pen a novel.

- One post should equal a solution. Remain focused on one idea and don't stray from it. The more specific, the better.

- Get to know your readers better and figure out what problems they might need help with.

- Make sure your ideas are validated before you spend money on ads. It is best to test ideas on a small scale and then add in paid ads later, instead of spending money not knowing if it will pay off in the long run.

- Find what content brings you the most profit. Focus on getting more page views to those articles and create more like these. Your goal shouldn't be on page views but on page views to the pages that bring in the profits.

12. Robbie Richards

His blog earnings are over $5,000 each month. He brings in this money through affiliate revenue and he doesn't spend one penny on ads or other traffic strategies. He has been able to boost his traffic by 402 percent, monetize his email list, get over 4,000 subscribers, and increase email sign-ups seven times. Here are some tips from Robbie:

- Utilize smart links to change the opt-in forms that you show to a new reader and an existing subscriber. This allows you to show new readers an opt-in subscription form while showing an existing customer an app coupon, webinar, or new e-book link.

- Use a lead magnet for pages that get a lot of traffic. This lets you put all your best offers on one page.

- Use Thrive Content Builder to change up your landing page by using the "Upside Down Homepage" technique. This will put your opt-in form at the top of the page in banner form, where it will get the best attention.

- Change the subject heading on your emails and then resend the newsletter to anyone who didn't open it the first time.

- Place your post near the top of your Twitter page. Use an automatic scheduler and set it to post on your social media platforms multiple times during a month. Change up your hashtags and taglines.

- When you relaunch any updated content, change the published date, too. Reach out to people who commented, shared, or promoted the article before. Tell them about the update.

- Use subheadings and headlines that are catchy and state the benefits that the reader will get.

- If your posts are long, reformat them into articles that are more readable. Break up long paragraphs into three-or-four-sentence snippets. Add in media or images per 100 words and have a clickable table of contents.

- Re-publish, update, and optimize posts that already exist that correspond to your keywords.

- Use sorting techniques, conditional formatting, and filters to help you sift through keywords.

- Do a keyword search for existing content and find which ones show up more. Any words that rank between six and twenty and have an average of 300 hits per month are what you want to choose.

Aim Higher: Setting New Goals

Being human, we are bad at thinking about compound growth. We like to think linearly. We like overestimating the things we can achieve in a short amount of time but we underestimate the long run. Setting the right goals lets you tie your big ambitions with your daily tactics so you won't get in too deep but it won't let you sell yourself short, either.

Let's look at some methods you can do now to take your blog to the next level. We will look at the main components of goals that are workable, and how to form and develop them. I'll also show you how to implement these strategies, putting them into practice, sticking with them, keeping track of your achievements, and some roadblocks you might encounter.

13. Begin with "Why?"

The main question you have to ask yourself is: "Why did I create this blog?" What do you want to achieve by running it?

If you blindly pick and choose a goal, it will make it harder for you to find the drive to achieve it. Take some time and write down some outlines or ideas that you think should be the purpose of your blog. Then figure out where you want to take your business.

14. SMART Goals

Once you have the wherefores and whys out of the way, let's figure out how to set effective and manageable goals. These will make sure that you are targeting improvable, specific areas and you are setting yourself up for long-term, sustainable growth.

The SMART system has been used by many to set goals. You might have heard about it, but let's look at it in depth. SMART is a checklist that makes sure you are able to attain your goals in the best way possible. SMART stands for:

- **Specific**: You have to narrow down your plans to specific goals. If you don't, you won't know whether or not you are succeeding.

- **Measurable**: You have to be able to measure your goals so they can be effective. "Being a better writer" can't be measured, but "Writing a post that gets one hundred shares" can be measured.

- **Achievable**: You might eventually get 10,000 people to read your blog. But you can't expect this in the first month. You have to begin small and work your way up. Focus on what is possible or you are going to be very disappointed.

- **Relevant**: You have to make sure your goals are relevant to why you are creating a blog.

- **Time-bound**: The best way to ignore anything is not to put any time constraints on it. Having the goal of "writing ten blogs" has a different urgency than "writing ten blogs by November." When you put hard limits on your time, you will make sure that you have a purpose to do things now.

What do **SMART** goals look like when blogging? Let's split them into three types of goals:

- **Optimization goals**: these will relate to how you understand the process of making goals:

  - "Set up Google Analytics for the blog and check these numbers weekly and update the results on a spreadsheet."

  - "Read and take notes on four main articles during the next two weeks."

- **Performance goals**: these will relate to how your blog is doing:

  - "Increase email sign-up rates by twenty percent in the next three months."

  - "Publish more blogs this quarter than last quarter."

  - "Increase traffic by ten percent in one month."

- **Creation goals**: these will be about creating targets for your output:

  - "Publish to a new market, like a podcast or a video, to reach new audiences."

  - "Create three new blog concepts."

  - "Write five hundred words every day for one week."

Look back on the list you created earlier. You should be getting a sense of how you can take those ideas and turn them into SMART goals. As a starting point: take those ideas and develop five concrete goals from them.

15. Following Through

By now you should have a notion about the type of format you need to use for your goals to make them effective. What can you use to achieve your goals? Let's look at some obvious points first:

• Never create too many goals. It would be better to reach a few goals than to fail at ten. Build on your successes and make it a priority to use what works for you, instead of trying to succeed at all things.

• Write down your goals and place them where you will see them every day, so you are motivated to reach them.

• Figure out what you aren't going to prioritize. Create clear boundaries between what you are and aren't going to worry about when you are working toward a certain goal. When you can set boundaries, you are removing any interference that might cause you to feel like you are failing.

• Create goal triggers. Instead of telling yourself to write each week, try to set a goal of writing on Tuesday after you eat lunch. This goes back to the "time-bound" section of your SMART goals. This can help you establish concrete and routine times to work on your goals.

16. Review Process

You will choose and then keep track of the most important goals, whether they are quarterly, weekly, or daily. This will make it easier to set smaller goals and lets you work more effectively on small tasks.

The biggest benefit of this is avoiding traps to respond to what is urgent rather than what is important. This helps you prioritize your blog content. Most of these things are completely unrealistic with the amount of time they demand of you. So how does this review process work?

- For example, when you are working on quarterly goals, you need to work on three blogs for the next thirteen weeks. Look back at your last quarter: your failures, achievements, and accomplishments. Do you need to adjust any goals? Now, create goals for the next quarter and narrow them down.

- Setting weekly goals is very similar. You just break your quarterly goals down into shorter time frames – for example, weeks one through five, or six through ten. This should only take you a few minutes.

- You shouldn't have to set any daily goals, but use these same principles when you are working throughout the week. Create three "to-dos" when you are working on your blog, and base them on your weekly goals. This is an effective way to make you focus on what is important.

17. Track Your Achievements

It is very important that you keep track of your goals and achievements. Humans don't do well at keeping a lot of different thoughts in mind at one time. This is why we write things down. Make sure you have your goals written down, to keep you organized and motivated. It is very satisfying to look back at your goals and seeing everything that you have achieved.

Keeping track of your achievements is just one way to keep yourself accountable. There are many ways to keep track of these; you just have to figure out what works best for you. The best way to make sure you stick with your goals is by external accountability. There are many ways you can do this:

- Be accountable to a lot of people by posting updates on social media about your progress toward your goals.

- Up your personal stakes by using a service like stickK or Beeminder. These use a "nudge" theory to motivate you to stick to your goals.

- Talk about your goals with friends or family at least once a week.

- This part of reaching your goals is easy to skip because it takes time. Since you are working on your blog instead of "in" your blog, it is important when trying to make progress.

18. Common Roadblocks

Most people don't make goals because most of the time life happens and we don't reach them. You have read this book this far, so you are trying to improve your life and learn new things. You have already overcome one hurdle: you haven't given up.

Just because you set a goal once and it didn't happen, doesn't mean you won't ever reach a goal. Here are three common roadblocks that most people encounter when they set goals, and how to stay away from them:

- Setting too many goals at one time. If you think about it, you could set 100 goals to help you improve. But if you try to do them all at one time, you are going to get overwhelmed and find that you can't achieve even one of them. Three is the best number.

- Setting goals that aren't focused on. It is great to begin blogging – but what does it really mean? Do you want to strike up a lovely discussion on a specific topic? Do you want your thoughts and ideas to be expressed by talking or writing about them on various sites? Would you like to be a guest writer on other sites? Why do you want to do these things? You have to focus.

- Setting goals that are unrealistic. If you tell yourself that you will reach 10,000 views in one month, this isn't achievable if you aren't already a well-known writer. You can't beat yourself up just because you are getting only 100 views each month when other blogs are pulling in a lot more.

What you have learned by now should help you figure out what is wrong, and ways to solve these problems. The main thing you have to do is set a few, achievable, focused goals, and then stick with them. If this sounds a lot like common sense, it is. We have been told to "dream big" and that is usually our first impulse.

The main thing is to not ever give up. You need to focus on slow growth that will compound. Tie these to other goals and you will begin to see results.

Chapter 2: Blogging Secret #1: Content Marketing

Now that you have decided to start a blog, it is a good time to think about what the future might hold for bloggers and the content marketing world. Upcoming trends indicate that blogs are going to continue being popular, but the content that is created and the way people produce blogs will constantly evolve.

In this chapter, we will be covering the most profitable niches, the dos and don'ts of blogging, hacks, tricks, and content tips, email marketing made simple, and proven strategies.

Niche is King: Profitable Niches Revealed

Blogging is the main type of content marketing and each is very integrated. A great blog will focus on three metrics: good design, regular publishing, and quality content. Editing support and collaboration is just as important as using media such as audios, videos, and images. Research and updates could help build your authority and leadership about your chosen blog content. If you want to use content marketing strategy as a way to make money with your blog, you need to learn the trends, facts, and statistics.

The best niches are the ones that offer profitability, demand, and fulfillment. You could think about niches as what to major in when going to college. Courses like computer engineering and finance make sense if your priority is to earn a large salary. Teaching or being a social worker could be fulfilling but they come with a lower salary. Neither one of these options is wrong or right. What is important is you have to know what you want. After that, you can pick a niche that will be in alignment with your goals.

You can't become a teacher if your main priority is to bring in a six-figure income straight out of college. If you want to make money with your blog, you can't pick a niche that is hard to make money from. This sounds obvious, but it is a very common mistake that many people make.

It doesn't matter if you have been blogging for a long time or are new to the blogging business, what is important is to give serious thought to which niche to choose. Let's look at the three main factors when picking a niche:

- **Profitability**

  - The best blog ideas are ones where you offer great value to others by helping a lot of people solve their problems. Now, you need to figure out if your idea will be profitable. This is very easy.

  - You just have to ask yourself this question: "Do other bloggers make money in this niche?"

Competition is a good thing in the blogging world. There will probably be many blogs on whatever niche you decide to enter into. It is easier to make money in larger niches, since companies have realized how powerful blogs have become as a marketing tool.

There are many opportunities to make money with:

- Advertising.

- Sponsored content.

- Affiliate marketing.

The main questions you need to ask when picking your niche are:

- Do bloggers make money in this niche?

- What could I make that can offer the best value to others?

•Demand

Creating value is about helping others. What you make that gives the best value to a large number of people will maximize demand. A common trait that many blogs share is they help solve problems. This does sound simple. Solving problems is creating value. When you can help others solve their problems, you will have a better chance of success.

•Fulfillment

Everyone is familiar with the saying: "Follow your passion and success will follow." This advice is always given freely but it could be quite dangerous if you follow it. Your passion will come after you have worked hard to get excellent at something that is valuable. So, basically, what you do is not as important as how you do it.

If you ever want to love what you do, you have to get rid of the mindset of: "What can the world offer me?" You need to think: "What can I give to the world?"

Let's begin here: "What can I make that will give the largest value to the world?"

This mindset will put you on the path to fulfillment and it will give you the biggest chance for success. You have to find things that you are passionate about so you can find the niche where you can give the most.

If you have a lot of experience in a certain field, this is where you can provide the largest value. Expertise and experience aren't required. If you just have something that you are passionate about or something you are going through that you think will resonate with readers, write about that. Your blog can be about when you solved a huge problem, or just sharing your journey.

Most Popular Niche Ideas

My goal here is to help you find better ways to save and make money. Let's look at the most profitable, proven blog niches along with the cons and pros of each. All of these have already passed the test and they will make you money. You will need to narrow the choices down within each niche.

1. Travel.

In order to have a great travel blog, you need to:

- •Know how to get traffic from SEOs and social media.

- •Inspire others to get out and enjoy life.

- •Have a certain audience to build content for.

Basically, none of these points should be surprising to you. Creating content, SEO, and social media around a certain demographic is what makes blogs successful.

Cons:

- • Larger up-front costs for travel.

- • There isn't a large opportunity to sell expensive products to this kind of audience since people's budgets usually go to their travel expenses.

- • Most blog content revolves around traveling, so you need to be able and willing to do a lot of traveling now and in the future.

Pros:

- • It is fun.

- • Great potential to make money by referring credit cards.

- Create content that is linked to niches that are related to travel hacking and making money when traveling.

2. Multi-Niche or Lifestyle.

It is easy to create a blog that is based on a niche. The main trend you can't ignore is the dozens of multi-niche blogs that have been successful and are taking the blogging world by storm. These bloggers create a content strategy about what interests them.

If you take a deep dive into successful multi-niche blogs, you will see that their content is extremely calculated and usually focuses on creating content that can drive traffic through Pinterest.

Successful multi-niche blogs will focus on solving issues around a certain demographic. A millennial lifestyle blog might focus on relationships, career, travel, and finance. Mommy blogs might focus on cooking, cleaning, home life, and parenting.

Cons:

- Your audience might have a different problem that your blog doesn't cover and this makes it harder to come up with a content strategy.

- It might be hard to rank on Google if your content is broad instead of more deeply focused on one topic.

Pros:

- More money-making opportunities.

- Keep things interesting if you get bored with certain topics.

- You can switch up topics based on new trends.

3. Fitness and Health.

The biggest benefit of the fitness and health niche is that these readers are hungry for information. People are looking for answers to their questions and they want them "yesterday." It would be great to use Pinterest for this niche. It will be easy to build a lot of traffic to your blog. Many fitness and health blogs make money by using affiliate programs. The bloggers who make the big bucks have products that will solve their audience's problems.

Cons:

- Seasonal – usually peaks around January.

- This topic is very competitive.

Pros:

- Makes money in various ways: from expensive products to affiliate revenue.

4. Investing and Personal Finance.

This is my favorite niche of all. There is a huge demand on Pinterest for topics that deal with saving money and living a frugal life. Because of this, you could build traffic fairly fast while creating an SEO strategy at the same time. The biggest money-making blogs focus on making money (shocker) because this is obviously what people want to know.

Cons:

- It is a competitive space within search engines and most large publishing companies will fight over this traffic.

- It can be seasonal. Interest usually peaks between November and February.

Pros:

- Information on how to manage finances and make smart investments is in high demand.

- Can turn into a money-making niche when you have a large following.

5. Fashion.

This niche is extremely visual. This is good, since social media is becoming more visual, with highly successful sites like YouTube, Pinterest, and Instagram. Affiliate marketing, sponsored content, and display ads are the most common money-making strategies.

Cons:

- Not great for trying to sell expensive products.

- Your brand is visually based around you.

Pros:

- Many opportunities on less competitive and visual networks like YouTube, Pinterest, and Instagram.

- It is possible to make money with affiliate programs selling accessories and clothing.

6. Food.

Food bloggers make money through advertising. This means you have to generate many page views before you will be successful with your blog. You can do this fairly fast by having a good strategy using Pinterest. There is a lot of competition in culinary areas like vegan, keto, and paleo. If you are interested in this niche, do tons of research beforehand, using "Google Trends." Try to find a trend that is just beginning to gain some traction. It would have been a great time to begin a blog focusing on paleo during 2009.

Cons:

- Most people want to find free recipes, so you normally can't sell products.

- It is a labor of love to create new recipes. You have to test them, take pictures, and write all the content.

Pros:

- New trends usually emerge extremely fast and this can create great opportunities if you can react fast enough.

- There are many brands in this space and this lets you use sponsored posts.

- This topic is in high demand for both social media and search engines.

7. Crafts and DIY.

The largest niches on Pinterest are do-it-yourself (DIY), crafts, arts, and sewing. Because it is easier to get traffic to new sites via Pinterest, compared to Google, you could build a very successful blog extremely fast.

Cons:

- Hard to sell expensive products.

Pros:

- A wonderful visual niche that has huge potential on YouTube.

- Can sell products on Etsy or Shopify.

- Huge potential on social media and search engines: especially Pinterest.

8. Marketing and Business.

An old proverb says: "In the land of the blind, the one-eyed man is king."

This is basically saying that if you compare yourself to others who have no skills in a certain area, even having a small level of skill puts you in a stronger position than the competition. This is an important concept to remember when you want to get into the most competitive niche: marketing and business.

If you want to begin a blog that deals with making money, you are going to be competing with the smartest bloggers in the world. But let's say, for example, you actually begin a blog about marketing specifically for freight brokers – a niche industry that finds carriers to ship freight. Here, you are the one-eyed man in a room full of blind people. This is what you want to be, metaphorically speaking, and where you will most likely find success as a blogger in the competitive scene of marketing and business blogging.

Cons:

- This is a field that is crowded and you will be competing with some bloggers who have more experience.

Pros:

- You will sharpen your marketing and business skills.

- You can sell expensive products along with consulting services.

Bottom Line

If you are thinking about beginning a blog and you know you have a great niche in mind, the only thing I can say is to do it. You aren't going to know everything about the topic today, but when it comes to blogging, you actually learn on the job.

Mastering Blog Posts: The Dos and Don'ts

Would you like to know how to write a blog post that will convert? Do your posts convert the way you want them to? We are going to cover some tips that will help you write blogs that will convert.

You might see that many people who visit your blog usually leave without reading it completely. What's worse is that more people who see your post on social media, like Facebook and Twitter, won't even click on it.

You only have about two to three seconds to grab a person's attention and convince them to click on and read your post. How can you make sure your marketing efforts aren't being wasted? If you follow these tips, you will soon be writing posts that will convert.

- **Call-to-action**

You have to add a clear call-to-action. It doesn't matter if you ask your readers to purchase something, follow you on your social media accounts, share your post, or leave a comment, just be sure you state what you want them to do clearly.

This needs to be something that stands out and is easily distinguishable. You could say something like: "If you like this post, then I'd like it if you would share this on Facebook and Twitter."

- **Optimize SEO**

I don't recommend that you write for SEO, but it doesn't hurt to keep SEO in mind while you write. Google searches drive a large amount of traffic for many websites. If you want to maximize your ranking on Google, you need to optimize your posts for the most important ranking factors.

Here are some tips to keep in mind:

- Interlink content.

- Add images.

- Use variations of keywords.

- Optimize the focus keyword.

- Add in the right meta description.

- Add in the right meta title.

- **Images**

The human brain will process visual content faster than just words. This is why you need to add images that captivate audiences and that will help engage others. There are many free resources that offer free images.

- **Bullet Points**

Everybody will skim down a page before they read it, so you need to highlight your most important information. Bullet points are great, since they are easy to see and skim. Here are tips to use when writing bullet points that people will stop to read:

- Express your clear intent. Bullet points are miniature headlines.

- Don't clutter your bullet points. Don't write paragraphs.

- Keep the bullet points symmetrical. Try for no more than two lines.

- **Subheadings**

Getting your formatting correct is critical for blogs. There isn't anything worse than reading a blog that is one huge paragraph. Most people will just skim through before they read the whole post. It is recommended that you break up the article by using subheadings. Whatever you can do to make it easier for the user to read your blog, so they will take any actions you might want them to do.

- **Headlines**

If your headlines aren't compelling, there will be a good chance that your post won't be shared; much less read. Humans are shallow people. We are constantly judging books by their covers and blogs by their titles. This is why it is critical for your blog title to be compelling, or your blog won't be successful. You could use a headline analyzer to find how valuable your headline will be. This can also give you tips on ways to improve the headline.

- **Know Your Target Audience**

Before you even begin writing, you have to know who your audience is going to be and the things they want. Rather than guessing what your audience wants or needs, do some competitor analysis and industry research. It sounds complicated, doesn't it? Good news, it isn't.

There are many resources you can use and here are some I use frequently:

- SEMRush: this one you have to pay for but it works great and lets you spy on your competitors so you can steal their ideas.

- Quora: This is a great resource to find questions that people are asking within your niche.

- Twitter Advanced Search: all you have to do is type a keyword and then select a filter question. It will then show you any and all questions that people are asking in your niche.

- KeywordTool.io: this is a free tool that lets you see the most popular keywords that people are using in your niche.

I hope these tips are helpful to you. If you can follow these, you will be writing blog posts that successfully convert.

Content Tips, Tricks, and Hacks

Content marketing is a powerful tool that creates serious results. It's a great way to build trust, generate leads, and increase your sales. It's a strategy that any business or anyone who is on a budget can use and benefit from. You might be sitting there thinking: "Been there, done that, it isn't for me." You might just be exploring the idea of content marketing and aren't sure where you should start. It doesn't matter. I can personally tell you that it will work to grow your business and it doesn't have to be complicated. All you need to know is where you have to focus your efforts.

Content marketing is a tool that requires patience, effort, and depending on your preference, it might take some budget or time. Even though it might take some work, many businesses both large and small continue to prioritize content marketing above most other business strategies.

The reason they do this is that they have figured out how to achieve huge results with a very minimal investment. The best way to make content marketing work for you is to be focused on what brings in results, so you don't waste time on things that don't work. It sounds simple, but you have to pay attention to the details.

Here are some tips that have been proven to help you transform your content into the ultimate marketing tool:

- **Start with the End**

The best way to create a plan is to work backward. Before you begin any type of content, you have to be completely clear on what your marketing goals are, and what you want to accomplish. This will shape and streamline your message. This gives each piece of content a purpose.

If you want to generate leads, you will need to brainstorm on content that gives quick wins and will entice visitors to give you their email address. If your goal is increasing sales and you are working farther down the funnel, you may want to think about having a webinar that will showcase your services and products. This creates brand awareness. Then you can check out being a guest on a podcast or hosting your own. Every piece of content will bring prospects closer to being a loyal customer.

- **Know Your Customer**

It will be useless if you create content that your target audience doesn't care about. This totally defeats the purpose of content marketing. All of your content needs to hinge on understanding and knowing your audience. Visualizing your ideal customer avatar is a great way to know that you are creating the perfect content. This perfect avatar needs to include information such as interests, geographic location, profession, and age, so you can get a sense of the type of topics and problems that impact your ideal readers' lives the most. You can leverage this material to make your connection with your audience deeper, by using content that resonates with them. When they feel like you understand them, they will begin to trust and like you. You will need to keep this avatar handy for the next tip, too.

• Salt in Their Wounds

Nothing makes a person want to act more than pain. It doesn't matter if the pain is physical, emotional, or financial. When somebody is hurting, they will be in the market for something that will make the pain go away. You want to stay away from using dramatic or cruel tactics here, but the point is to bring awareness to the discomfort and follow it up by offering a solution.

Look at your customer avatar and see if you can identify their largest "pain points." Use contrast to create a picture that is specific to what life might be like on the other side of their troubles, then offer your services and products as the vehicle to get them there. Could you free up some time so they can eat dinner with their family? Will you give them the confidence they need to approach their boss about a raise that was promised? How could you make their life more productive, brighter, or happier? Use your content to solve their problems.

• Respect the Platform

Your content needs to look like it belongs, and not seem out of place. This means that you have to respect whatever platform you are using, and study what form and style of content works best there. The best way to do this is to look at what other successful bloggers are doing on their platform and then see how you could adapt, customize, and unleash your own version. Also, don't ever be afraid to look outside your niche to get some inspiration.

• Go to Them

Many valuable resources go into making and distributing your content. If it attracts little or no response, it feels like you have wasted money, energy, and time. It will discourage you from moving forward, so you need to do everything in your power to make sure your content doesn't fall on deaf ears, by picking channels and platforms that your market actually uses. This might sound like common sense, but it is easy to get sucked into using a million different social media sites, just because they seem popular today. Do some research and figure out where your market hangs out online. By putting your content on platforms your target audience uses and prefers, you will improve your chances of reaching them and you will stay away from hitting dead ends with your content.

• Share and Syndicate

After you have created some content, don't be afraid to carve it up and share it on other platforms and channels. For example, a video could be turned into a podcast episode, which could be transcribed into a blog post. You could even carve it up more into tweets, Facebook posts, or condensed into articles for LinkedIn. Syndicating your content across other channels is a great way to extend your reach to potential customers who wouldn't have heard of you. For example, somebody who listens to podcasts might spend less time reading blogs. A daily Facebook user might never have a reason to go on LinkedIn. Using some minor tweaks to optimize and freshen up your content for various platforms will stretch your money and reach.

• Call-to-Action

You have just given your audience a huge dose of quality content. Now you need to take the opportunity to help point your prospects in the right direction. So, provide them with the next piece of the puzzle. You can do this by ending each piece of content with a friendly call to action like this: "If you want to discover how to easily turn your marketing strategy into high converting and profitable content, without spending hours stuck at your desk staring at the blank screen of death wondering what to write, then I highly encourage you to download your FREE copy of [whatever you have to offer your customers]."

With all the marketing options out there, content marketing can deliver higher quality leads and customers than just about any other strategy out there. In fact, the marketing institute says that businesses that use content marketing have six times more conversions than businesses that don't. So, get started today by working on applying these tips to make your content marketing more efficient and effective. By doing this, you can provide top-notch value to your customers, increase your impact, and watch your business grow.

Email Marketing Made Simple

You have written an awesome blog post. You have published it but to your horror, no one has read it. Why? Did you promote it with email? If not, why didn't you?

Email marketing is the most effective method of communicating directly with your readers. Encourage people to sign up to your email list with opt-in pop-ups, RSS feeds, and social contests. Then create and send emails to drive a ton of traffic to your blog.

Here are some tips that will help you drive traffic to your blog:

- **Visual Newsletters**

Most people like visual information. You can entice your readers to click on your blog with newsletters full of images. Add-in summaries of articles that let the audience know your main points but end each one with a tease and a clickable button that says: "Read more here."

Don't send out too many newsletters. Your readers have lives, too. Monitor the opened and click-through rates from the emailed newsletters, to figure out the best times and frequency to send your newsletters.

- **Scheduling Articles**

Create a scheduling calendar for your articles to be published. This makes it easier for you. You will be able to keep track of when you need more content.

Sending regular articles to people who have signed up for your newsletter will keep them reading your blog. This creates a habit for your readers, deepens their trust in you, and makes you feel more familiar to them, as they get to know when to expect your next article. You need to schedule your articles in advance.

- **Call-to-Action**

You have to be clear in your emails about what you want from your readers. If you want people to click through to your blog, you have to ask them. You will increase your response rates if you do.

You also have to make it easy for them to act on your request. Make sure the link to your blog post is easy to see and is clickable. You can create colored call to action (CTA) buttons that are embedded in your email. You could use a formatting site like MailChimp, Fusion, and Stamplia to make your CTA buttons easier to create. These are highly effective, so don't forget to use them.

- **Segmenting Emails**

You need to segment your email list into more targeted groups, based on what your business needs. Send out your newsletters and blog articles to people who actually read it. You could even create various emails and newsletters and link them to the same article.

If you are sending an email to a business supplier, you want to send them different emails than the ones you are sending to your customers.

- **Personalize Notes**

You need to keep your emails personalized. Include names and other personal details that you know about your email subscribers. If your articles are related to their business, mention the business name, and how your post is going to help them. Personalizing emails will increase the click-through rate by about thirteen percent.

- **Get Real**

To get people to click through to your blog, make the email content real. Impersonal, corporate, or stock emails aren't going to get any results today. You have to remember that you are competing with thousands of other emails in a person's inbox.

You have to write your emails as if you are sending a message to a friend. Use words like "me" and "you" in the content. Create a tone that will resonate with your demographics. Make sure it is professional but at the same time conversational.

Deepen the relationship with your subscribers by keeping it real and inviting them to join you on your blog.

• Subject Line

The subject line of your email can make or break you before anyone ever reads your message. You have to take the time to create a good subject line. Make sure it is short but to the point and don't forget the "call to action". Convey a great benefit, a state of disbelief, a sense of urgency, or ask questions in your email.

Test your subject lines and find the ones that are getting opened the most, read, and clicked-through, and use this information to improve them in the future.

• Email to Get Emails

You have to use your email to get in touch with many people. Use your signature to get people to click through to your blog. Create a friendly call to action in the email signature and invite contacts to visit your blog. Add in a brief benefit to motivate some action. Tell them what your blog is about. Don't forget to include an easy link to click.

• Opt-in Pop-ups

I know that newsletter pop-ups are annoying but they can also work to increase your subscribers. They actually work so well that most bloggers, whether they are single bloggers or corporate bloggers, will use them.

Implement the pop-up efficiently by placing it correctly and by using a pop-up builder. Give reasons for why visitors to your site need to have your newsletter, and how your products or services will make their lives better. Use words like "exclusive content" or "free" and keep the tone friendly, and you will get more people to sign up.

- **Create RSS Feeds**

Make it easy for people to keep in touch with you once they have visited your site. Create and set up an RSS subscription button on your site. Make sure it is a contrasting color and make it visible close to the top of the page.

- **Generating Social Email Tips**

There are many effective and cool ways to get people signing up to your email through social platforms. You could include a link on all your social media platforms that will take people to your blog. You could post content like coupons, e-books, and webinars. You could also make Facebook tabs full of exclusive offers and incentives.

- **Get Leads from Campaigns**

You have probably hosted campaigns like sweepstakes and contests. Most businesses do. Social contests help you spread your brand but they are also a way to get more emails. Have a sweepstake on your blog, Twitter, or Facebook. Ask for people's email as a way for them to enter.

You can also motivate people to spread the word about your offer by doing a referral campaign: this gives them deals for telling their friends to give you their emails.

Proven Strategies: The Blog Niche That Made $100k in 9 Months

Jeff Rose spent nine months constantly blogging before he even made his first $100. That equals about 17 cents an hour. Can you imagine working a full-time job and only making 17 cents an hour? You would have quit on your first day.

Jeff didn't quit, he learned from his mistakes and began a new site, where he made over $100K in only nine months. Let's find out how.

Jeff realized that there were ways to use Google AdSense, banner ads, and affiliate marketing to make money. He decided to see what all the fuss was about, and began networking to find people who could show him how he could make money with his blog

Once Jeff began making money, he got the idea to begin another site. On his new site, he talked about insurance, investing, and financial planning. He figured out that one area he was getting paid a lot through Google ads was with life insurance. Using Google AdWords, Jeff saw which life insurance companies and marketers were willing to pay per click just to have their ads displayed on websites and Google searches. He knew that if insurance companies were willing to pay anywhere between $25 to $50 per click to have their ad displayed on a person's website, they would be willing to pay more per lead. He wondered how much he was missing out on when it came to life insurance commissions, since he was giving it away through Google ads and only getting a pay-per-click.

Since Jeff was a financial planner, he was able to sell life insurance products, such as term life insurance. He decided to try to sell term life insurance policies through his site, rather than just making money with pay-per-click. He started a journey of making phone calls and eventually found an insurance brokerage that focused on online leads. Through talking to them, he found there was tons of revenue out there that he was leaving behind. He was shown other insurance blogs and sites and how well they were doing, including one particular site that was bringing in around $50,000 per month. When Jeff realized that, he said to himself: "I can do that."

Using the website GoDaddy, Jeff registered his new domain name. He had his website, he had the motivation, and he knew he could make money from this site. Now, he had to figure out how to create the content and get people to actually go to his site and then want to give him their email address or call him for a quote.

He did keyword research. He used the tool called SEMRush and he still uses it today. This tool lets you find competitive keywords from various sites that you might be tracking. He checked out his competition to see what kind of content they were producing so he could replicate it on his site.

During the time he was getting his new site running, Jeff was also working as a financial planner, he had his old site that he was still blogging on, and he had a family. He had a lot going on in his life and he didn't have a lot of time to put into this new site. He wanted to make sure he could outsource as much work as he could and still get the best results. So, Jeff decided to use an app called Mobile Assistant where he used his cell phone to transcribe his blog and then it was typed up within 48 hours and emailed back to him. He then put this on his blog. This app does cost money per month but it is worth it.

Jeff also decided to outsource some of his writing. He advises that you do the research and find a site that will give you quality work. Don't just use a company because it is cheap. Use one that will give you the high quality work that you need and want. You will pay more money for quality but if you want a successful company, you are going to have to pay out some money to bring in customers.

Jeff published quality content and promoted that content on all the social media sites. He offered various types of media. He created podcasts and put them on various social media sites that backlinked to his life insurance website.

The best thing you can do to create a great blog is to do a huge amount of research on keywords and be well educated in your chosen niche. You have to network and just work hard. It is important to use social media to feed into your main blog, and the more media you can offer, the better off you will be. You have to be willing to call, email, and keep in touch with people who have visited your site in order to make money.

Chapter 3: Blogging Secret #2: Setting Your Mindset

You can use affiliate marketing to help your blog make money for you. I will teach you the basics of affiliate marketing, along with some strategies, networks, how to use Amazon, etc. Read on to find out everything you need to know about affiliate marketing.

How Affiliate Marketing Can Work for Your Blog

Affiliate marketing is where you get money from promoting somebody else's program, service, or product. You promote whatever it is by providing your readers with a special link on your blog. When they click your link and then buy a product, you will either get a percentage or a specified rate for that sale.

It is a win-win for everyone involved, with these benefits:

- A person who buys the program, service, or product gets exposed to something that is beneficial or helpful that they might not have known about.

- The person or brand that has the program, service, or product will be getting more sales that they might not have gotten on their own, so this is making more money for them and more of an impact on their company. This makes them happy to give away some profits.

- You are sharing helpful resources and information with your readers that will improve their lives, plus you are making money.

You should only promote services or brands that you have tried, trust, and love. The affiliate needs to be in alignment with your personal mission or philosophy.

You may have to turn down some sponsors or affiliates due to questionable business practices, ingredients, or you might not like their product after you've tried it.

In order to run your business with integrity, you can't be in it just for the money. I would like to make money, but nothing beats my audience's experience. You need to make sure you are delivering valuable content that is interesting, whether or not your visitors buy something from one of your affiliates. Your number one priority is to weave affiliates into your content and to be transparent and authentic in whatever you are promoting.

7 Affiliate Marketing Strategies All Blogs Must Follow

Now that you know how affiliate marketing works, here are some strategies that every blog needs to follow.

19. Add links to posts that perform well.

Go back and find the posts that were the most popular and weave affiliate links into their content. If you are still getting traffic to these posts, then it would be great if you can make money from those engagements.

You need to make sure that the links feel natural and not like you are placing promo links just "anywhere."

20. Make videos for your top affiliates.

It would be a great idea to add helpful videos to your affiliate posts. Most bloggers know that videos are extremely popular right now. Videos can help show the buyer what to expect if they do decide to buy what you are promoting. If it is a great program, service, or product, seeing it in action will make them want to buy it.

It's just like scrolling through Facebook and seeing a cooking video that makes you stop and watch. You get sucked in and think, "Wow, I can do that." Before you know it, you are running to the store to buy the ingredients to make that recipe.

If you appear in the video, it will make your audience more familiar with you. You want your audience to feel comfortable around you. You want them to trust you and feel like they know you. Sometimes there isn't any better way to do this than a video.

21. Make dedicated posts for your top affiliates.

Your readers will buy a product faster if they see the value that it brings into your life. The best way to show them this is by a dedicated blog that details one affiliate and all the reasons why you love them, including ways these products will make the reader's life so much better.

You can do this with review style posts. When a person reads about something, the more they are likely to think: "This sounds helpful. I think I will try it."

You only need to do this for your top affiliates, since it won't be worth your time and effort to make blog posts for affiliates that just bring in a couple of bucks each month.

22. Make a resource page.

You might be familiar with a "resource page," since most blogs will have them nowadays. Basically, it is a roundup of your favorite courses, subscriptions, apps, services, or products that you think your readers will like, too. These are things that you get value from. These will be your best performing affiliate links.

Don't stop there. Many people tend to have only one resource page, but you can have as many as you would like. If you have multiple niches, think about breaking up your content into many pages that have been targeted to cover specific niches, versus only one page that is general.

23. Place affiliate links on social media.

There are many different social media sites out there, so why not use them all?

- **Twitter**

You can tweet about why you love your affiliate. Remember to tag them and use their affiliate link. It's that simple.

- **Facebook**

You can post videos and photos of your affiliates on your page, with an announcement about time-sensitive enrollments or sales for your affiliates.

Videos are wonderful: you can do unboxing videos and put it on various channels; you can create a tutorial or video about a certain topic and then link it to products in your Facebook shop in the caption. You could even do a Facebook Live and mention any affiliates if you think it is appropriate.

- **Instagram**

You can add affiliate links to your stories, your favorite things, your highlight reel, or static posts. You don't need to overdo it, because you want to stay authentic and not have your feed look like thousands of billboards.

Adding links every now and then is a great way to reach more people while sharing helpful recommendations.

- **Pinterest**

You can "pin" things that will either send your audience to a direct link where they can buy a product, or to your blog post where you have written about your affiliate.

You should have pictures so you will stand out, and where you can, offer a discount or special deal by using a link.

Make sure to schedule these posts by using Tailwind.

You need to remember that on all social media platforms you have to use #affiliate for transparency, or indicate the affiliate relationship when posting an affiliate link by saying "thank you" beside the link.

On all platforms, you can use "share threads" to get engagement with your videos and posts. This will help show the algorithm that people like your content and this will help expand your reach.

24. Put affiliate links inside emails.

You can follow up regular emails with a wrap-up weekly email where you can remind people about what you loved about that week, along with some updates on new blog posts.

On Sundays, you can send out a list of emails where you include some affiliate links for services and products that you love and are currently using. These emails need to be personal. You need to talk about your life, you, and what you are loving, feeling, reading, eating, and doing.

This list is meant to give your readers value, while building your relationship with them and earning their trust, so you can inspire others to live a better, healthier life.

This means that three times each week, you have the opportunity to make money from affiliate marketing, while also providing your readers with product recommendations and value that could solve a problem they might be having in their life. Plus, you can give them tricks, tips, and fun updates.

25. Send emails that highlight one affiliate company.

Once your readers have signed up for your emails, you can officially begin sending them emails.

Pick a day of the week that works best for you and send out an email that features only one affiliate service or product that you are currently using and have fallen in love with. It might be a new product or just one your affiliate is promoting. Just make sure you have tested and tried this product and can give a true recommendation. You can also choose a new affiliate, so you can see how interested your readers are with them.

Make sure that these emails are just promoting one thing, so you don't distract your readers or give them too many calls to action. If you give a reader too many choices, they usually don't make any.

Give your readers ways to opt-out of emails. Be realistic, some people will get annoyed and won't want to get all of your emails anymore. Make it easy for them to opt-out of certain emails. You want to keep your people happy.

Some email systems don't have this functionality; ConvertKit makes this very easy to do.

Affiliate Marketing Networks: Which One?

Let's find out how to find the right affiliate network that will work best for you and your niche and we aren't talking about Amazon.

- **ClickBank**

ClickBank isn't just another affiliate network. It is a marketplace for affiliates and people who create products, so people can make money together without having agreements or a lot of paperwork.

ClickBank is a middleman between people who create digital products like music, videos, and e-books, and people who want to sell these products.

Being an affiliate marketer, you can create your unique affiliate link for thousands of products and begin to drive traffic to begin making money. You get to see your earnings in real-time.

It is free to join and there isn't a screening process. There aren't any complicated metrics. It is just a simplified network that is open to anybody who wants to try it.

- **ShareASale**

This company was founded in 2000. It is an affiliate network from Chicago, Illinois. ShareASale will pay a commission to affiliates based on their sales. You can choose from over 2500 programs that let you earn commissions.

The website features over 2500 merchants that offer many different services and products. Being an affiliate, you will select any of the merchants and try to make direct sales to their websites. The merchants will then pay you a commission for the sales that resulted from the affiliate's referrals. You get to decide the merchant that you would like to promote and ways you would want to promote them. You can log into the website and check the merchant's earnings and stats in real-time.

- **AvantLink**

This company has been in business for ten years and it is still improving its platform. AvantLink has been recognized as the fastest-growing entrepreneurial business in its field. It constantly strives for excellence and has an intense focus on quality instead of quantity.

If you have joined an affiliate network and later didn't like it, AvantLink removes this problem by giving you detailed overviews of all the merchant's programs before you join. By doing this, you don't have to worry about signing up for its program. You will be able to see information about the company, its products, and its affiliate program. This is the best feature for new affiliates who are worried about jumping into a program.

- **Rakuten Marketing**

Formerly known as LinkShare, Rakuten Marketing claims to be the largest affiliate marketing network out there today. It offers e-commerce, securities, banking, travel, e-books, media, and online marketing services.

Rakuten Marketing's system is always learning, in order to constantly bring customers into better focus. By analyzing its data, the company has a good understanding of consumers: where they are going, where they have been, what they value, and who they are. These insights, along with multi-channeled data, allow for intelligent optimization across all campaigns, for better effectiveness. The company gives its clients complete visibility and access to its platform.

Rakuten Marketing works with over 150,000 publishers around the world, as well as the biggest brands. Intelligence and insight get shared between publishing partners and advertisers and their joint success comes from working together.

- **CJ.com**

This company was previously called Commission Junction. You can find thousands of products on its website to make money off of. This affiliate is great for bloggers to connect with affiliate programs that get offered by thousands of online brands. The best part is that you don't need any exclusive training to learn how to use this network. Just sign up for a free account and begin exploring.

After you have signed up, complete your profile to make sure you get fast approval for CJ's affiliate program. Now, you can click on links to search for your niche or you can click on categories to browse new programs. You get paid through a check or by direct deposit.

- **FlexOffers**

FlexOffers will connect you with many reputable brand name companies that you can be an affiliate for. It has over 12,000 affiliate programs and adds new ones every day. FlexOffers has a wide range of programs for just about every niche out there.

To sign up, just go to the website and begin. Even if your blog is just beginning to grow, you will still be able to join, as long as you explain how you will promote products. Be as detailed as possible about your traffic sources, this gives you a better chance of being accepted into the program.

- **OfferVault**

This affiliate marketing website can find you cost-per-action offers from more than 60 affiliate networks.

Categories get listed for every search term that you enter, along with all of the relevant information on those offers made by the merchants. You will find all the offers that are available for your niche, so you can compare them to other networks.

OfferVault earns money by collecting monthly fees from the network for listing their offers.

Amazon Affiliate Marketing Made Easy

To make sure that you do well using the Amazon Associates program, let's go over some of the best tricks in the business.

1. Place links to products within your content.

Most income made from Amazon's affiliate program will come from basic text links. This means that you will hyperlink certain words in your text that people can click on that will take them to a product page on Amazon. You want to make sure this fits in with your niche and what you are talking about in your blog post. It's going to seem really odd if you are talking about losing weight and then you have a random paragraph that says, "Hey, check out this cool drone."

2. Turn images into clickable affiliate links.

Of course, the image should be of the actual product. These are the next best affiliate links to use on your website.

3. Add links to Amazon as often as you can.

The more links you have on your site, the more likely somebody will be to click on them. Don't wait until the very end to place your affiliate link. By the end, they should have been given numerous opportunities to click through to Amazon.

4. Product reviews do the best.

Doing some quality product reviews of things that relate to your niche is a great way to get a higher click-through rate and more sales. You want to make sure the review is very high quality, though. Ideally, you will want to get in contact with the company and have them send you a demo item to do the review on, but this takes more effort and won't work if you are just starting out. You can still do a review on things that you have actually bought and used.

5. Work during the holidays.

When do people buy the most? During the holidays. One Amazon affiliate made between $550 and $1000 each day during the week after Thanksgiving. Not all holidays payout this well, but typically you will make more money during gift-giving times of the year.

6. Place a "Buy Now" button in your posts.

You can do this easily with the EasyAzon plugin, but if you don't want to spend the money on that, you can insert a button yourself and make it an affiliate link.

7. Post articles about recurring deals.

If you want to be able to share posts about products that are on sale more often, the best way to do this is with a "weekly deals" post. So, you will publish a post each week with the best deals for items within your niche and then use all of the other tactics that we have covered.

8. Do a monthly bestseller list.

Amazon keeps an updated "bestsellers" list, so all you would have to do is post a blog each month and mention their list.

9. Just get people to visit Amazon.

One affiliate says that 30% of her earnings come from people who made a purchase on Amazon and she happened to be the person who sent them to Amazon. For example, she said that through one of her links, she sold a $5000 watch and made a $400 commission, but she doesn't have a website or link that talks about watches. When a person goes to Amazon from one of your links, you will get a percentage of whatever they buy for the following 24 hours, or 30 days if they add something to their cart. So, all you need to do is get them to click on one of your links.

Proven Strategies: The Amazon Affiliate Website That Makes $20k/Month

For this case study, I want to introduce you to 10beasts.com. This company has figured out how to make big money with the Amazon Associates program. Luqman Khan, the guy behind this website is big into technology, and it originally started out as a top 10 website.

When you go to the site, you will notice that it is very simple. It doesn't confuse you and it is very straightforward. It also only has about ten to fifteen pages. When you click on a post, there is a well-defined sidebar, which is something that is becoming obsolete in a lot of website themes. Another thing Luqman has figured out is how to keyword his title. The way he does that is by frequently using the year in the title: it gives him access to untouched traffic, and he updates his product reviews each year.

He also makes sure that he uses the main keyword of his blog post several times throughout the post, and definitely within the first 100 words. He also links out to other authoritative websites.

When it comes down to showing the list of the best whatever-he-is-talking-about in his post, he uses a table instead of listing things. Everything on the table is hyperlinked to another place in the article where you can read more about it, and he has the link for the Amazon page. All of the tables he uses can easily be created through plugins with WordPress. He also makes sure he shows the pros and cons of items, because people want to hear the truth.

So, he has figured out the best way to draw people in through the use of good keywords, and then he provides them with amazing content. This means that he has more people clicking through on his Amazon affiliate links and purchasing items. The great thing is that they don't have to buy that specific item for him to get the commission. As long as they buy something after clicking on his link, he gets a seven percent commission on the sale.

Chapter 4: Blogging Secret #3: E-Commerce & Dropshipping

The next way you can make money with your blog is through e-commerce or dropshipping. These require a more hands-on approach and you will definitely have to spend some money. This is also a type of monetization that won't work for everybody. There are some blog niches that simply don't provide you an easy item that you can sell. For example, if you choose a niche in finance, selling actual products is probably not a good idea. You could sell other things like books and classes that you create yourself, which we will talk about later, but you can't dropship or outsource items. But, if you are blogging about sports, then you can easily sell sports equipment. So, we're going to take a look at the different ways to get started with e-commerce and dropshipping.

Shopify Hacks You Need to Know

For most people who decide to get into e-commerce, Shopify's embedded capabilities helps to meet all of their needs. First, though, everything we are going to talk about in this section applies to every other section in this chapter. How you can use blogging to help your

Shopify business will help you with any other e-commerce or dropshipping business you create.

Shopify's embedded capabilities are also free and easy to start using and can help you get the most out of your store and your blog. First, you have to add your blog to your Shopify account. Go to the admin area and click on: "Online Store." Then choose: "Blog Posts." Then you will click: "Manage Blogs" and then: "Add Blog." You will then fill in the title of your blog. You can also have multiple blogs on one Shopify site.

Now you can write your blog post. You want to keep it relevant to your Shopify store. As we have talked about a lot, keep it contained in a niche. It will attract shoppers and keep them coming back.

Then you need to decide how you are going to manage your comments. You can either disable them, moderate them, or let them be automatically published. I would suggest moderating them. This means you have to approve them before they get published. This cuts down on rude comments and spam.

You also need to pick the right tags. This is how readers are going to find your blog. Then decide which social media buttons you are going to allow. They include Instagram, Pinterest, Twitter, Facebook, and others.

So how do you get people to come to your Shopify store? Here are a few tips:

1. A referral program.

You can generate traffic and sales by putting together a referral program for your store. An easy way to do this is with Shopify Affiliate Software. You can provide people a link to promote your site through online platforms and email.

2. Image SEO.

You can optimize your images to help them show up in searches more often. You will want to make sure that your images are properly tagged for social media and they should be compressed so that it improves the speed of the page. Shopify gives you the ability to edit image names and text so that you can create compelling descriptions.

3. Test prices.

You can split-test prices (also known as A/B testing) on Shopify for free and this is one of the best ways to figure out what people are willing to pay for certain items. Having the wrong price can end up sinking your store before it has even started. Using the Qbot Shopify app gives you the chance to split test prices, but you should plan out your tests over a certain period of time instead of testing everything all at once.

4. Trial run.

Have an idea that you can't wait to get started? You can see how well it will work on Shopify for free. Their store builder provides you with a free fourteen-day trial, but make sure that you have your supplier and stock sorted out. You can get the store up and running quickly, and during those free fourteen days, you can figure out if it is going to work for you or not.

5. Digital content.

Shopify also allows you to sell your expertise. So, if you don't want to sell physical products, you can sell digital downloads like webinars, e-books, worksheets, and so on.

With this in mind, go check out Shopify and see if it will work for you, (but after you have finished reading the rest of this book.)

Dropshipping Tips and Tricks

You may or may not have heard the term dropshipping before. If not, it is simply a way to sell things without having to have physical products on hand. You post things for sale on eBay or Amazon, and when somebody buys it, you go to another site and place the order for the item and put in the other person's shipping information. The dropshipper then sends the item to the person who bought it. But there is a little more to it than this.

The biggest plus with dropshipping is that it doesn't require any upfront investments. You don't have to buy products until somebody buys something from you. This may make dropshipping sound like it is a zero risk, high-reward business, and it basically is, but there are some risks associated with it. So, let's move into the risk and reward of dropshipping.

Advantage #1: Zero Capital Required

You can start a dropshipping business with zero money because you don't have to buy any products.

Advantage #2: Work Anywhere

You don't have to have a physical location, and you don't even have to be at home. As long as you have your phone or computer, you can work from anywhere.

Advantage #3: Scalability

It doesn't matter if you are selling phone cases or large pieces of furniture, the amount of work you have to put in is going to be the same. All you have to do is give your supplier the order information. The only limits are the limits that your supplier has.

Advantage #4: Endless Number of Products

Since you don't have to purchase any products, that means you can offer a wide variety of products and allow your sales data and blog posts to drive your business.

Disadvantage #1: High Risk

While you don't have to invest money, it is still high risk. The physical aspects of your business will be completely out of your hands. While you still have to tell your customers that you have stock, quick shipping and handling, and high quality products, you don't have any real control over these things. All of this is controlled by your supplier. It is common for a person to sell something and then go to their supplier to find out that they are out of stock. Most people will plan for this and have more than one dropshipper if this happens. But it is a risk that you might not be able to plan for.

Disadvantage #2: Low-Profit Margins

It doesn't take too much to get started with dropshipping, so it has become a very crowded business model, especially over the last few years. This means sellers have to be able to stand out in order to generate substantial revenue. But, you are starting with a blog, which may be just what you need to stand out from your competition.

Disadvantage #3: Slow Shipping Times

Shipping times are one of the biggest factors buyers look at with online shopping. Before you know it, Amazon will have drones delivering everything to people in about an hour. When you dropship your orders, the dropshippers will ship a lot slower than if you have control over it.

Alright, now that you know the advantages and disadvantages, let's move into the different types of dropshipping.

1. Dropshipping from suppliers.

This is the most common form of dropshipping. There are various suppliers that you can use, and you can negotiate your business deal before you start to list their products on Amazon or eBay. This way, you can establish a relationship with an actual supplier, unlike working with AliExpress. But finding a good supplier can sometimes be hard. It can take months to find the right supplier for you. There is also a lot of room for error.

2. Dropshipping from online retailers.

This is what is known as the arbitrage dropshipping model. The seller will take a look at the prices of items on different retailers, typically either Overstock, Target, Walmart, AliExpress, eBay, or Amazon. Let's say somebody finds an item for sale on Amazon for

$50 and the same item on eBay for $60. He would then exploit this arbitrage and make a profit by selling it on eBay and ordering it from Amazon.

This doesn't require you to establish a relationship with actual suppliers. When the person buys something from you, you go to Amazon and place the order and ship it to your buyer. This form of dropshipping is not very sustainable. Competition drives the price, so prices have a chance to change drastically in a short amount of time. Plus, this form of dropshipping kind of looks bad. A person orders something from eBay but then gets something in an Amazon box. Most marketplaces are trying to get rid of this form of dropshipping, so this may not be a good idea.

3. Dropshipping with Amazon FBA.

With this type of dropshipping, you would ship a bulk supply of your product to Amazon's warehouses. Amazon stores the product and then ships it out when a person orders it. You can also sell on other sites using Amazon's Fulfillment by Amazon (FBA) account. This incentivizes sellers to make sales on Amazon through a discounted shipping and handling rate. This isn't purely dropshipping, though, because you will need to purchase the product beforehand and ship it to Amazon's warehouses.

How Do You Start?

You don't need to quit your job first. Start your dropshipping and blog business on the side, and then once you have become established and are making revenue, you can quit your job. For example, Pierre Omidyar, the founder of eBay, didn't quit his job as a programmer until eBay generated an income that was more than his salary.

It's okay if you have zero experience, but you should still know the basics of bookkeeping, finances, and business registration. This will keep you from running into any problems once your business starts to take off. You don't have to do this right off the bat, but as soon as you have started to make about $500 each month, you should take some time to look into these four things:

1. Create the simplest form of a business in your country. For the US, this is a "Sole Proprietorship."

2. Create a business credit card and bank account.

3. Create a business PayPal account.

4. Learn e-commerce bookkeeping or find a professional to help you.

When it comes to finding products to sell, the best place to turn to is Alibaba.com. Here you will find lots of different suppliers and products. You can contact several suppliers about the same product and figure out which one is willing to give you the best price. Once you have decided who you are going to dropship with, and hashed out your deal, then you can list the item for sale on whatever marketplace you choose. You can also make a marketplace on your website.

Be ready for questions. People will want to know more about your product, so you will need to know how to answer their questions. You may have to go back to the supplier and ask them. In fact, I would suggest doing just that, so that you give your customers the right answer.

Once you make your first sale, you have to place your order with the supplier. The first time you do this, you may be afraid of screwing something up. You will go back to your supplier's site and send them the agreed-upon money for the item and give them the shipping information for the buyer. Once they get the money, they will send the product out to the buyer. You will then want to let the buyer know their order is on its way.

One last piece of advice for dropshipping is to go with products that have a price of $100 to $300. This gives you the biggest profit margin and people feel more comfortable buying things in this price range. Any higher, and people may think they are getting ripped off, and any lower, people may think the quality is bad.

Masters of the Marketplace (eBay, Amazon and More)

The next way to make money through e-commerce and your blog is to use different marketplaces. These include eBay, Amazon, and many more. Some people who sell on these marketplaces don't have a blog, while others do. To get the most from marketplaces, it is best to have a blog, because it is a great way to drive traffic to your stores. Linking to a store on another site is also cheaper than paying for a web page that has a store. Let's look at some ways to master these various marketplaces.

Most people will source their products from China, and this can take some time because you will want to get samples and see who has the best quality products. But the first thing you need to do is figure out what your first product is going to be. I'm going to share with you three product ideas. These are by no means the only options you have, and your products will also depend on what your blog niche is, because you want to make sure that they go together.

The first product is silicone ice cube trays. This product has a lot of revenue coming in. The top sellers of this product are bringing in 30k each month. It should also be easy to import and it shouldn't cause any problems. There is also a gap where people are having a hard time with their lids staying on the trays, so you could find a better quality product to offer. There are also products you could start selling that fit with this.

The second product is moth traps. Again, they have a good amount of revenue, not as much as the last product, but still averaging around 9k each month. Moth traps are also small and light, so this product is easy to import as well. There is also a gap that you can fix by improving upon the trap itself. It can also be easily bundled with other products.

The last product is a collapse laundry basket, which also has healthy revenue. These can also be easily shipped because they are collapsible. There are also ways to improve these.

As you can see, when it comes to figuring out what to sell, there are three main things you need to think about. First off, is the product going to make a decent amount of revenue? Second, how easy is it going to be to import and ship? Third, is there a way that you can improve things so that you can stand out from the competition?

Now, you are probably wondering where you can find your products to sell on eBay and Amazon. As I've said, most people will source their items from China because they can get them for a lot cheaper there, which gives you a bigger profit margin. But you don't have to source from China.

There are some people who simply go to places like Goodwill. Yes, I said Goodwill. If you've not been, it's a secondhand store where you can find clothing, houseware, and electronics. The crazy thing is, you can sometimes find unopened items and clothing that has barely, if ever, been worn. Other types of thrift stores are also a good idea. These places get leftover products that didn't get sold, and they sell them for less than half of their regular retail price.

Another option is to go to flea markets. You'd be amazed at what you can find at flea markets. There is a lot of stuff you may have to sort through, and there are people who know what they have, so you won't be able to talk them down in price, but sooner or later you will be able to find things that you can resell for a profit.

You can also look for online and brick and mortar shops that are having a sale or even going out of business. These are great times to stock up on items and still be able to make a profit on them when you resell them.

Now, remember, we're talking about making money through your blog. The first thing you need to do is figure out what things you can sell that fit in with your niche blog. When you do, you can funnel your readers to your shop on Amazon or eBay by placing a call-to-action at the bottom of all of your blog posts. As long as you make sure that you share calls to action regularly, and you constantly remind your readers about your shop, you can easily make money by selling on eBay or Amazon.

Etsy: Shine at Selling Your Own Products

Unlike the other e-commerce outlets that we have talked about, Etsy requires a more hands-on approach. Etsy is where people share their handmade items and various services, which range from clothing to tarot card readings. But getting sales is most of the time the hardest part, and that is where your blogging comes in.

Blogging to market your Etsy shop is one of the best ways to market for Etsy, instead of spending money on Etsy ads that may not work. I'm going to be honest with you right now; a lot of people will tell you that making money with your blog is easier than making money on Etsy. But, having a blog will enable you to make more Etsy sales. Here's an example of how a blog can help out: let's say a woman has worked hard for two years to establish herself on Etsy and is making $2500 a month in sales, so she decides to take a vacation. When she comes back, she switches out of vacation mode and all she gets is crickets. She is no longer making the sales she has made before.

Now, if this same woman had a blog, things would work a little bit differently. Before she heads out on vacation, she sends a message out to her readers letting them know what she is up to, so they know what is going on. Then, instead of turning off vacation mode as soon as she gets home, she sends out some messages to her followers. She tells them about her vacation and how she bought some supplies and is starting to make a new line for her Etsy store.

She chooses to put together a giveaway on her blog and other social media sites. In a week, she messages her readers asking if they want to be a part of her giveaway. The giveaway is a huge success. Once she picks a winner, she holds a flash sale for everybody that entered the giveaway for two days. A third of the people who entered buy something during this time. So instead of hearing crickets when she comes back from vacation, her shop is up and running again.

You can't rely on Etsy to make you successful. You have to go where the buyers are, and this means social media and blogs. You tell them through those outlets about what is going on with your Etsy shop. But when you choose a blog, you are basically creating a trap for shoppers. You have created one place where people can go to get updates from you, which is easier than them having to chase you around on several different sites.

You have their complete attention on your blog, and you post things that relate to the products you sell on Etsy. Here are some examples of Etsy sellers who became successful because of their blog.

A woman named Dana Fox created the blog called Wonder Forest. On Etsy, she sells phone cases and accessories. On her blog, she shares life hacks and tips in order to make your life fun and easy.

Liz Marie created a blog where she talks about interior design. On her Etsy shop, she sells vintage décor.

As you can see, blogs can make an average Etsy shop successful, and help you to bring in more money without a bunch of extra work on Etsy.

Proven Strategies: How One Woman Makes $40k/Month on Amazon

In this success story, one woman went from working a job and going to school full-time, to making around $40,000 each month on Amazon. It all started for her when she and her boyfriend took a class called ASM. This class sparked something inside of the woman to start an online business, mainly because she could do it while still working and going to school.

When it came time to pick her first product, she decided to go with something lightweight and affordable, because she didn't have extra money to spend on something big. She chose a konjac sponge, which is a beauty product. She did pretty well selling this product. She also did all of the other aspects of the business herself, like her business logo design and so on. The anonymous woman in this example says she only invested around $300 in this first product. She sourced this item from China, where each unit only cost her ten cents.

This first product had made it to $3,000 a month in earnings, when she started to think about her next product. Instead of focusing on the long-term at this time, she was just looking to see what would make her the most money. With time, she learned to look long-term and focus on building a brand that she could take off of Amazon and sell on her own website. Her trendy second product was 3-D fiber mascara. It brought her $5,000 a month.

At this point, the woman knew she wanted to go for a product that would bring in more money, instead of products that can be sold at a cheap price. Her advice is to go with something that is worth more than $20. This will give you better product margins. Plus, it gives you a better chance of making the product unique.

With time, she started having problems getting her products because she was sourcing them from China. At one point, her product got caught up in customs for a month, which hurt her on Amazon because she didn't have anything to sell. So, she made a transition to where she is now. She looked at Amazon and tried to figure out what she should do differently, using herself as an example to figure out what consumers bought on Amazon. The woman realized that waist trainers were the main thing that she bought on Amazon, and it was a very specific niche.

As she made this move, she started to look at ways to save herself money and make sure her business wasn't damaged by returns. That's when she turned to social media to market herself and make sure that people measured themselves before they bought her product. She turned to YouTube, and this helped her create traction, because she kept everything very niche and focused on waist trainers. She also used Facebook and has a private Facebook group for people who have bought her products. She used these social media outlets to save money on ads, and the more people she attracted to these outlets, the more sales she started to make on Amazon.

She also made sure her product was better quality than was otherwise available on Amazon. It was also a product that she trusted. With her faith in the product and her social media marketing, she was able to up her sales on Amazon, until she reached $40,000 a month. She has now expanded and started her own website as well, and she suggests that should be something people aim for when it comes to e-commerce.

Chapter 5: Blogging Secret #4: Expert Info-Products

The next way we are going to look at making money with your blog is through selling info-products. This means you are going to have to establish yourself as an authority figure and then create something that people will want to buy to learn from.

Sell Your Expertise

Before you start trying to sell info-products, you have to show you are an expert. It doesn't matter whether you feel like an expert or not, you have to make your possible clients feel as if you are, otherwise, you won't sell a thing.

Some fields have qualifications that show people that they are an expert. For example, you could be a registered dietician and that automatically makes you seem like an expert in diet and nutrition. Other areas of expertise aren't so easy. But right now, I want you to think about the people you view as experts in your chosen niche. Now, what if you had the combined knowledge of these people? This doesn't mean knowing everything they know, but having a general understanding of the topics they cover. Would you feel as if you were an expert? Probably.

Write down those people who came to mind, and then write down their most important works. Once you have figured out their body of work, you will choose a couple of those to focus on. This is the knowledge you need to learn. Take some time to study up on these things, and make lists or mindmaps to help you learn the topics.

You don't have to be able to quote everything that is covered, but you do want a decent understanding of the information. You want to understand it enough that you can confidently answer questions about it.

Then, start putting yourself out there. Publish regular blog posts and diversify the content that you share. Start looking to get added to speaking events. This puts your face out there as well. An important thing to remember is, once you start becoming more popular and more established, don't become arrogant. You want to stay tasteful and respectful. If you start becoming cocky, condescending, or rude, you will lose your status as an expert.

Lastly, make sure you create original content. I understand that almost everything has been covered before by someone else, but you can put your own spin on things. Make sure you never plagiarize another. You can let others inspire you, but always come up with your own blog posts and so forth.

Kickass Info-Products and How to Sell Them

So, you want to monetize your knowledge. Well, the first way to do that is through info-products. Basically, an info-product is something that has been created from one or more sources to meet a certain purpose. The format of these products can be video, audio, written, or a combination of all of them. These are the seven main types of info-products:

1. **E-books** – These are digital books that people can read on devices. This is a type of passive income, because all you will need to do is promote it once it is published.

2. **Phone applications** – These are apps that people use that allow them to interact with information. This requires a lot of technical know-how, or you will have to hire a person to make it for you, which can cost a lot. It could, however, make you some passive income, depending on what your app is about.

3. **Membership sites** – This is a website people pay to be a part of to get regular content that they can't get on the free version of the site. This requires a hands-on approach and is not a form of passive income.

4. **Virtual summits** – This is like an online conference. A person will get access to different webinars and videos created by various experts. This will take time to put together, and requires a more hands-on approach. This does not make passive income, because it takes place at a certain time.

5. **Webinars** – Short videos that are shared live that focus on a small part of an expert's bigger picture. They can be replayed at any time when a person purchases access to the webinar, so this makes passive income.

6. **Online courses** – This is a course that has been created that people can take online to learn about something. It takes a lot of time to create, but it makes passive income once it is up and running, requiring only promotion.

7. **Workbooks and templates** – This is another book that a person can fill in. It is structured in a way that helps the customer learn something. Again, this involves passive income, only promoting is required.

Now you have to figure out which type of info-product you should create. To figure that out, ask yourself these questions:

1. How much time are you willing to spend on creating your product? And how much effort? An online course takes a lot more time than a webinar.

2. Do you want to make one thing and sell it over and over, or do you want to create content on a regular basis?

3. How much money do you want to bring in versus the effort?

4. How much experience and knowledge do you have in your niche and do you want to partner with other experts?

5. What does your audience want and are they already buying things?

6. How many tools do you know how to use and are you ready to learn new things?

So how do you sell these products online? Here are some important steps to take to do so:

1. Who is the target market and what problem are you going to help them solve?

You will see this time and time again in this book, but it is the first step on almost everything you will do, when it comes to monetizing your blog. You must stay within your niche, so within that, who are you going to try to sell to and what is it that they need help with? If you are in the fitness world, are you selling to people who need to lose weight, or people who need to bulk up? Those are two very different types of people, so you have to know your target market and what they need help with.

2. Research your competition.

Look to see what is already available for your target market. Then you will need to figure out how you can position yourself within all of that. ClickBank is a great place to see what is already out there, and it is a place where you can sell your products as well.

3. What is your big idea?

This is what people are going to be paying for. This is your promise, so to speak. Going back to the fitness example, there are lots of different big ideas that you can share. Maybe you have a workout plan that helps bodybuilders gain lots of muscle in a short time. Basically, you want to know what you are going to sell and how you are going to make that stand out against the competition, so you have to make it fun and exciting.

4. Come up with your product marketing.

Don't make the product yet. You need to sit down and figure out how you are going to market your product. This will include the benefits of your product and success stories that your product can bring. This is all how you are going to sell your product once you are ready to share it.

5. How are you going to share your product?

This is probably the most overwhelming step. This is where you need to decide how you are going to get your product out there. The easiest way to handle this without getting overwhelmed is to focus on a single platform at first. I would suggest starting with Facebook Ads because it is one of the easiest platforms to use and will bring you a lot of revenue.

6. Create your product.

Now you can make the product. Depending on what product you choose, this could take a few days to several months to do. But, I also want to say, you should have fun with this step. This is where you get to be creative, instead of dealing with all the technical parts. Once your product is created, you can launch on your chosen site.

7. Keep an eye on your sales.

Once you have launched your product, you need to keep an eye on the metrics and see how it is doing. You may find that you have to change your distribution avenues, landing pages, or ads. You shouldn't just "let it be" because that is the quickest way to lose money. Babysit it and adjust things as you see fit.

E-Book Launching and Marketing Secrets

Selling e-books is no small feat. One side of the playing field is people telling you it's easy and they made hundreds, if not thousands, of dollars overnight. On the other side are people telling you that you have to market, market, market and sales won't happen overnight. Neither one is inherently wrong or right. But the one thing the people who made money overnight aren't telling you is that they did market. They probably put a bunch of blood, sweat, and tears into their book and the marketing before it ever launched. This means that marketing is really the most important thing in making money with your e-books. We're going to look at some of the best practices.

1. Consider who your audience is.

The first thing you have to do is figure out who your audience is and what your book is going to provide them. This is going to also center around your blog niche. Remember, these are all ways for you to make money through your blog. If you are writing a blog about investing, then your readers are going to want a book from you that centers around investing and not a cookbook of your grandmother's favorite recipes. Also, think about how you are going to prove to your readers that they should trust the information in your book. How do they know you know what you're talking about?

2. Build a landing page.

Next, you've got to figure out how you are going to get people to actually see your book and want to buy it. This is where a landing page with a free offering comes in. You want to give them something of value and also be able to fulfill any promises you have or will make.

If you plan on staying in the blogging game, any form of deceit is going to end up costing you a lot. Word will spread fast that you don't deliver, and people will stay away. If you use MailChimp for your email list, this company offers a landing page of sorts. On that landing page, it needs to say something along the lines of "Sign up today and get my free ..." This free thing needs to be something your readers are going to want to have. Maybe you have some videos that you could sell as a free beginner's course about something. Or you could offer a PDF that includes helpful information. The important thing is that it will be something that your readers will actually find valuable, and they won't feel like they have been cheated, while you are also not giving away a lot of material for free.

3. Create a compelling call-to-action.

Think about your niche, how are you going to draw your audience in? If your niche is within the fitness and health realm, is there some secret workout that you have created or know about that few others know about? If you help with relationships, do you have some tools to offer your audience that they won't be able to find elsewhere?

This is what you are going to place at the end of your blog posts that have a link to your MailChimp landing page. This is how you are going to get people to sign up for your email list, so that they stay up-to-date and you have people to market to when it comes time to launch your book.

4. Create a conversation.

You have a growing email list now, so it is important to get to know those people. You now have to send them regular emails so that they know you're still alive. It's these emails that are going to help you build a rapport with them. Let them know about your upcoming articles, but also engage with them. Ask them questions. Things like, who are you, what things would you like to see me cover, or is there something that you are struggling with? This shows your readers that you care and that you want to help them. This will also help to build trust.

5. Begin writing your book.

This probably seems too far down on the list, but you want to make sure you have people to sell your book to before you write your book. Now, I can't tell you what you need to write or how to write it. That is all up to you. This is probably one of the hardest parts of the process, because for everything else you can follow a system others have used, but writing a book is something personal. It will likely take you months to do, and then you have to edit it. But, I trust that you can do this as long as you have figured out your audience and everything I asked you to do in step one.

6. Marketing your book.

This is the most important part. Now, you can do this through the email list you have created, and that's why we created the email list. If you are using MailChimp, you can come up with a campaign to send out to your subscribers that highlights different parts of your book and explains why it would be valuable to your subscribers. I would suggest making this a week-long campaign that goes all the way up to your publishing date. This will get you presales. It may also cost some of your subscribers, but that's okay. Not everybody will be at a point in their life to take a chance on you, so buying a book might not fit into where they are. But you should also make some sales.

Through these steps, you should have a solid foundation for creating and selling your e-book. It's also important to ask your readers to leave you a review if they liked the book. Reviews are what helps you place higher on Amazon. Then people who have bought, read and liked your book will share it with other people. This should become a snowball effect on the sales of your book.

Teach It: Selling Courses and Webinars

The next way to make money online by sharing your expertise is through webinars and courses. This is probably one of the hardest options because coming up with a course, creating it, and then selling it, can seem quite daunting. But I am going to talk about some of the best strategies to use to make sure you are able to successfully create and sell a course online.

1. Make sure you know what you want to teach.

This shouldn't just be an idea of what you want to teach or simply your niche. This means what you want to provide a person. What are they going to be able to do after your course that they couldn't do before it? Nobody has ever woken up one morning thinking, "I want to buy an online course today." No. That's not going to happen. People don't buy courses just to buy courses. They buy the courses to get a specific outcome, so you want to make sure that you know what outcome your course is going to give them.

2. Coming up with a good price.

This is probably the hardest part, aside from making the actual course. Most people will undercharge on their course, mainly because they don't think their information is valuable. Their content is just fine; they are simply lacking confidence. As a general rule of thumb, $100 should be the lowest you should price your courses.

This may or may not sound like a lot to you, but research has found that people are more likely to buy and finish an online course if they are priced over $100 than under $100. It goes back to the whole idea of: "You get what you pay for," as well as the fact that the more money a person has invested in something, the more likely they are to finish it. If you have a price in mind, chances are, if you double it, you will be closer to a good price.

A lot of people have undercharged and not done well, but when they go to re-release, they double the price and they start doing better. Another way to figure out the price is to double what you think it's worth and then add 50%.

3. Figure out what goals you want to meet with your course.

Now, the best way to sell your online course is to have an established email list. Those people on the email list should be people interested in your topic, and when you launch the course, you sell it to them. So, figuring out your goals will let you know how many people you need to make sure you have on your email list before you launch.

Here's an example of how you can figure this out. Let's say your goal is to make $10,000 in income. The conversion rate for the number of people who will buy from your email list is about two percent, and let's say your course price is $300. You then would take that information to figure out how many people you need on your email list. In this example, you would need 1700 people on your email list, in order to reach your goal of $10,000 at a two percent conversion rate.

4. Build your email list.

Now that you know how many people you need, you need to build your email list. There are a lot of different ways to build an email list. Basically, all you need to do is figure out what you can give away in return for an email address. You've seen things like this on websites, I'm sure. A pop-up comes up telling you if you sign up you get a free copy of an e-book or a free course. This is just one example of how to get subscribers, but it is a very effective way, because people like to get free things.

5. Come up with an outline and create your content.

While this may be what you want to start with, it should really be closer to the bottom of your list. You want to make sure that you will be successful on your launch before you start spending your time creating your content. Once you've made it to this step, you need to figure out an outline for your course. This is a very important step because you need to know the start and finish and how you are going to get there.

If your course comes out feeling unstructured, then people are going to be less likely to buy anything else from you, and they definitely won't spread the word. Once you have an outline for your course, then you can start to record your content. This can be a video or just an audio recording, but most people will prefer to have something to watch instead of just listening to you talk. Having visuals to back up what you are talking about makes learning a lot easier.

6. Make sure you pick the best software tools.

This applies more to webinars than online courses. Online courses are static. You simply upload them to a site where people buy them and then use the prerecorded information. For a webinar, it tends to happen live, and you want to make sure that it actually works so that people can enjoy what you are sharing and it plays all the way through without freezing.

There are some free and paid tools out there, and unfortunately, there will be some trial and error with this. But, I can suggest giving ezTalks Webinar a try. It has a lot to offer and you won't be hit with a bunch of extra fees that some software has. You can also attract people to a paid webinar by starting out with some free webinars from time to time. During a free one, you can plug your paid one and ask them to sign up, and if you have enticed them enough, they will.

Selling courses and webinars can be a very lucrative method of making money through your blog and with your expertise. It will take a lot of work, but it is worth it in the long run. You may also need to invest in some recording and audio equipment in order to make high-quality videos. In the end, if you use the tips provided, you will make your money back and then some.

Proven Strategies: How One Man Makes $40k/Month Selling Info

To round out this chapter, we are going to look at how one man was able to sell products and make $40,000 each month. He has used other monetization methods as well, like affiliate marketing, blogging, and Kindle publishing, but selling products has made him the most money.

When he sells products online, he is able to funnel the traffic and visitors that his blog gets into the products. Instead of simply being an affiliate for another person and only getting a commission, he gets all of the profits and is able to continue expanding his own business instead of another person's business.

The product he makes most of his money on is a course that teaches people how to make money using Kindle. He funnels people into signing up for his classes through all of his other sources, like the people who read his books or those who read his blog. He also uses affiliate marketers to help send him business, and he pays them a commission. He sells his course through a website called ClickBank, which also has its own affiliate marketing system. This isn't the only way to sell courses, though. Udemy is a popular place where people sell courses.

The man in this example explains that when he sells his course on different websites, like ClickBank, Udemy, and others, he tests different looks to see what works best. This is something that helps with every area of blogging. You want to attract people and not send them away, and having your site look nice as well as sharing enough information, helps to attract people. The man has found that placing a grid under his "buy" button with the recent purchases of his course has helped immensely.

Doing something like this, coming up with a course to sell that people find helpful and informative, will take time. For this particular businessman, it took him about six months to come up with his course. He also put $1000 into this course before he started seeing a return on his project. He suggests that people start out with selling Kindle books and being an affiliate marketer before trying to create a course like this.

Chapter 6: Blogging Secret #5: Advertising

We're going to round out this book by talking about advertising. This isn't advertising your blog, but instead, making money by placing ads on your blog. This is a very popular way to make money on blogs, and there are a lot of options, so everybody should be able to find a way to make money through advertisements.

Ads and Your Blog: Ways to Profit

The last way to monetize your blog that we are going to talk about, is through ads. Online advertising centers on three main forms of ads: pay-per-click, pay-per-impression, and pay-per-action.

Contextual ads are often pay-per-click. These ads are shared based on what you write about. In theory, the ads should match up with the content of your web page, which increases the odds of a person clicking on them. Google AdSense is the most popular version of this.

Text ads that use a hyperlink and are separate from the main content of the blog post – but which usually still have keywords matching the blog's theme – are known as text link ads.

Impression-based ads pay the blogger based on how many times their ad appears on their website.

Affiliate ads are ads that link people with relevant products on another website. The blogger gets paid when a reader clicks on the link and buys the product.

Then some bloggers use direct ads, which means they allow visitors to purchase ad space on their blog. These often show up as banners or other types of display ads. The pricing varies with each blogger.

Then you have sponsored reviews and sponsored posts. Reviews are indirect forms of ads. Companies will sometimes get in contact with a blogger to ask them for a review of their services, site, business, or product. Similar to this is the sponsored post. These line up with the content of a blog post, and are mentioned in a natural context. If a blogger is writing about baking, they may mention and share a link to their favorite mixer. The vendor will then pay the blogger for the mention.

All of the revenue from these various forms of advertising depends greatly on the traffic to your site. It is important that you have already worked hard to increase your traffic before you jump into ads, otherwise, you might be disappointed with what you make.

Direct Advertising: Mastering PPC, CPM, and More

Selling direct advertising is a solid way to bring in some money every month. This means that you place ads on your website for other sites, and they pay you to do so. There are many different forms of direct advertising that you can use, so the possibilities are endless. Now, before you start trying to make money going down this route, you want to make sure that you have enough readers. While there isn't a rule for how many you should have, try to shoot for around 50,000 page views before trying to sell ads.

There are six popular ways to make money through advertising:

- Paid reviews.
- Pop-ups.
- CPM ad networks.
- Sell text links.
- Sell your own ads.
- Pay per click.

1. Pay-per-click.

This is probably the most popular form of advertising. Pay-per-click, or PPC, or cost-per-click, or CPC, is an ad on your site that people have to click on. When they click on it, the advertiser will pay you an agreed-upon price. There are several websites that you can use to find ads.

Infolinks offers people a 70% revenue share and uses a PPC model. The in-text ads placed on your site are double-underlined words that will appear as ads when a person clicks on them. Infolinks also has InFrame, InTag, and InSearch ads. It offers payment options through Western Union and wire transfer once you reach $100, or through eCheck or PayPal once you reach $50.

Media.net is another option and is controlled by the Yahoo Bing Network. The ads that are placed focus on relevant keywords, so it will take some time before they match up well with your site. The more you use this platform, the better the algorithm will figure out the best keywords for your readers. Media.net also provides a dedicated account rep who can suggest more ways to increase your revenue through ads, and it uses PayPal or a wire transfer, with the payment minimum $100.

Chitika is another alternative for contextual ads and it offers a CPC program. The ads can be customized and they work well along with AdSense. The minimum payout is $10 through PayPal.

2. Sell ads.

You can sell direct ads on your blog and it places the control in your hands. The only thing you have to do is place an "Advertise With Us" page on your website and share the different types of formats of ads that you have available and how much it will cost them each month. You should also share your Google PageRank, Alexa rank, and any other traffic stats. But, you can save yourself the hassle of selling and use third-party alternatives.

BuySellAds is an ad-marketplace where people can place ad space for others to buy. You have to be a high traffic blog to post on this site, so if you are starting out, you will want to wait a few months.

3. Sell text links.

If your blog gets a lot of good organic traffic, you could try your hand at text-link ads. This is where you link a piece of text in your post to a page on another site. Before you start doing this, you should use a Nofollow tag to avoid a Google penalty.

LinkWorth is a text-link network where you will find options for paid reviews, text ads, and more.

4. Cost-per-click networks.

For the most part, we have covered the CPC model for ads. This means that you only get paid for ads if somebody clicks through. There is an alternative to this known as CPM, meaning cost per thousand, where you get paid for every 1000 impressions the ad gets. When it comes to CPC, the income can vary, but that doesn't happen with CPM. If the network sets the CPM at $5 then you will end up making $500 per 100,000 impressions, and so forth.

PulsePoint is a CPM network where you have the ability to set your price. To get accepted, you have to have a lot of original content. PulsePoint mainly sells to US-based viewers. When you come up with your price, make sure it is more than what you make with your backup. If they aren't able to pay what your backup pays you, then the backup is shown.

5. Pop-ups.

Most bloggers and advertisers steer clear of pop-up ads nowadays, but it is still an option. You can use pop-ups or pop-unders. A site you can use is called PopAds, and you can set your price and the frequency in which they happen for your visitors.

6. Paid reviews.

A decent amount of money can be made through publishing reviews for services and products that you trust and fit in your niche. The great thing about this is you get paid per review. Prices typically range from $150 to $500, but it all depends on your rank and traffic.

SponsoredReviews is a site that gives advertisers a chance to generate backlinks and a chance for bloggers to make money.

Some of these direct advertising options aren't even ads at all and are just sponsored reviews and posts. These are just a few ways to make money on your blog through advertising.

Become an AdSense Ninja

One of the most popular ways to start monetizing websites and blogs is through Google AdSense. AdSense basically gives the blogger a chance to add different ads to their site. When readers go to their blog and then click on an ad, the blogger makes money. Google will also take a little for themselves and then it sends out what is left to the blogger once a month. It is a very interesting way to make a little more money with your blog, but when you have the right-sized audience, AdSense can turn blogs into careers. But how can you be successful with this?

We're going to look at some ways to increase the revenue you make through Google AdSense, so that you can continue to make revenue throughout the life of your blog. We'll also round out this section by looking at ethical uses of contextual advertising, because using these ads ethically is just as important as using them correctly.

1. Properly place your ads.

The biggest problem people normally have when they first start out using AdSense is that they don't have a clue as to how to properly place the advertisements. There are a lot of different factors that you have to remember when it comes to ad placement.

First off, you should make sure that your ads are placed where your visitors will see them right off the bat. However, you need to make sure you balance out the number of ads so that they don't come off as annoying. Nobody likes going to those websites that have so many ads that it slows down the site and it's hard to find the actual content.

Typically, good ad placement will begin with placing a single long rectangular ad. You can also place a couple of ads on the right of the page for visibility. These ads can be 160 by 600 to 300 by 250. You can play around with the numbers within acceptable ranges to figure out what is best for you. Again, you have to make sure that you don't overdo things with the number of ads. Not only are your visitors going to get annoyed, but the more ads you have on your page, the less money you will make with each click. So, fewer ads mean that you could make more money.

2. Try to use high paying keywords.

Nearly every single niche within the accepted topics of Google will have "high paying" keywords. There are some topics that Google excludes in its AdSense, like tobacco. When you use high paying keywords within your article for your niche, you are going to receive ads that fit within that. When you have ads that match up to good keywords, you will make more revenue and get more clicks.

Figuring out what these high paying keywords are is easy. Google offers a keyword planner tool that is free to use and will give you the chance to search for several different phrases, keywords, or websites and figure out what keywords readers are looking for. You can also sort the information out by price so that you know which one makes the most money per click.

As you start working with different keywords you will start to learn what works best for your niche. There will be a lot of trial and error when you first start out because keywords and ads work together. As you start using different keywords, your ads will change as well.

You may find that you receive more clicks with lower value keywords, or might make more money by using the top keyword. Like with everything else, it will require tweaks as you start to develop your blog and use ads.

3. Change up the design of the ads.

After you have figured out the ads you will use, you can edit them in order to make them fit on your site. You shouldn't skip this when incorporating ads. Your ads should never stick out like a sore thumb. There are a few things to take into consideration when doing this. First, you want to make sure that you use colors and borders that match up with your website.

Then you should make sure that you use complimenting colors in the text and background of your ads. They need to stick out, but it shouldn't be in a glaring way. You want them to be clear and noticeable. If your website has a dark background, then you should use a lighter color so that the ad is noticeable. You should always do a preview to see if the ad looks natural.

4. Keep an eye on your results.

Too many people will upload some ads to their AdSense account and then forget about them. They don't check in on them each day, or even once a week. They just sit around and wait for money to come in at the end of each month. You can't make a decent amount of money if you don't check in on the ads to see if they are working for you. AdSense gives you the ability to track analytics on your ads to see what is working and what could use some improvement.

You should think about using a form of A/B testing. For example, on one of your blogs, you could place two ads and then three on another blog post. Then you can check in on the results each day to see which way is working better. If you discover that the post with three ads is working better for you, come up with another blog using three ads. Check to see if that blog gets consistent results. You then will need to continue to edit and tweak your ads until you like the money that you are making on your pages.

The sky's the limit when it comes to working with AdSense. Google provides bloggers with everything they need in order to be successful. If you also use other blogging tools, such as a lead list where you send out content, make sure you monitor the clicks you are getting on your ads regularly, and update those ads so that they will blend seamlessly into your site. There isn't a limit to how much you can make using AdSense.

Ethical Contextual Advertising

Knowing the best way to place ads on your site is one thing, but ethically using ads is another. This may sound like something I made up, or that it's not important, but you'd be surprised how often bloggers use some shady ad placement tactics. These tactics will also cost you readers and money. First off, let's quickly go over the four types of contextual ads that you can pick from:

- **Textual**: these are ads that link to other web resources without using modal pop-ups.

- **Pop-up**: these are ads that show a modal pop-up when the mouse moves over them.

- **Banner**: these are video, animated, or static ads that are placed in your posts.

- **Affiliate**: these are banner or textual ads that have affiliate codes in them that you earn a commission on when somebody places a purchase after clicking through.

All four of these types of ads can be used on your website if you would like. But we're here to talk about the rough side of content links, and these options have to be handled with care. This will help you to make some important decisions about the best display practices.

1. Privacy friendly or intrusive?

Script-based, dynamic ads like the ones provided by Chitika, Kontera, and InfoLinks are often intrusive to the privacy of the user because that not only tracks the clicks but the browsing activities and behavior of the user across your website and other web pages. Static links don't track users and are more privacy-friendly. Even if they do track, it is limited to the clicks and where they lead. There are two rules you should try to follow:

- Make sure that users give you "permission" to use dynamic ads, because this will make them more likely to accept the ads you have and they will feel as if you are trustworthy. This can be done through polls on your blog, mailing list, or modal dialogs that ask the readers if they want to enable ads.

- When using static links, place them where they make the most sense with your content and then diversify them through custom CSS so they don't look like your regular links.

Whatever you decide to do, make sure that you have a privacy policy where your users know what type of ads you have on your blog and let them know what the risks are for loading, viewing, and clicking on the ads.

2. Disclosure.

This tends to not be an issue for dynamic ads. The dynamic ad systems will normally automatically diversify ads from the regular links on a website. If your regular links are blue, then the system doing the dynamic ads may make them orange. When it comes to static links, it works a bit differently. The banners don't come with a disclosure. Plus, AdBlock won't recognize static banner ads as ads since they aren't script-based.

So, while dynamic ads come with their own style and a third-party disclosure, static ads will require you to add these things manually. You will need CSS styling to make them stand out from your other graphics and links. You will also need disclaimers on every page with these ads letting your readers know that there are ads on your site and what that means.

Not marking sponsored content, you will push your readers away, because they will feel as if they can't trust you. There are also laws that state that all advertising relationships have to be shared with the public.

3. Ad-blocker problems.

Business Insider released a report on ad-blocking in 2015 and it stated the number of ad-blocking users around the world had grown from 121 million to 181 million in a single year. This is a trend that worries the publishing and advertising industry. But viewers started doing this for a reason. Ad-blocking became more popular because websites had started to abuse the experience of the viewer. Nobody likes to be bombarded by pop-ups as soon as they visit a website.

I would suggest that you think about the types of ads that you are going to use and the reason why your viewers may choose to block them. The best way to figure out what your viewers would be okay with is to create a poll or survey and ask them if they are afraid of ads or they have ever clicked on a malicious ad.

If you choose to use dynamic ads, then you could use a cookie-based disclaimer that notices ad-blockers and shows a message to the viewer if they will allow ads on your website. If you have a WordPress-based blog, there is a plugin that you can use known as AdBlock Alerter that will do all of this for you.

To work around this problem altogether, you can choose to go with static ads with counters. This works for affiliate links and it won't trigger ad-blocking software.

4. Contextual ads and guest posts

Yes, ads should be used in your posts and guest posts, but you will need to figure out which, dynamic or static, will work best. Let's say you choose to use static ads and let's say that you let your guest bloggers include some products or affiliate links within their post. When you get asked to place a link to that post that matches the keywords of the writer, and the link takes the viewers to a competitor of the writer's brand, that writer will likely end up feeling betrayed and it could hurt your relationship with them. This is something you want to avoid.

If you want to use static ads, you will want to speak with the writer of the post first, letting them know and then ask if any conflict could arise. No matter what their answer is, you will have proven to the writer that you are trustworthy and they may end up writing more posts.

Dynamic ads put links into your posts automatically, so unless you add a "Guest Post" section and exclude that section from ads, or you reject the link, there is nothing that you can do. However, guest bloggers will likely already know that they are contributing to a site that uses dynamic ads. If, for some reason, they are not aware of this, reach out to them and inform them. Basically, make sure that conflicts of interest don't come up.

Backlinking Secrets: Ways to Profit Without Begging

It can be very frustrating to try and develop backlinks to your website. It is a process that requires dedication, patience, and work. We are no longer in the days of simple SEO where you can add any type of link into your site anywhere on the internet. In order for backlinks to be successful, copywriters and digital marketers have to be conscious of their backlink strategy.

Backlinks are one of the most traditional SEO techniques and they provide an easy way to increase search rankings and traffic. However, you only need high-quality links in order to generate the best SEO results and to boost your site traffic.

Ever since backlinks have become one of the most popular ways to boost a website's SEO ranking, Google has switched up its classification for backlinks and how they affect a site's rankings. So, nowadays, in order to build backlinks, site managers and owners have to make sure that they work to organically grow backlinks with time.

To simply explain backlinks, they are also known as external backlinks and they are another site owners link to a different person's website. They could place this link on a service page, a blog post, or some other place on their site. Backlinks are very important for SEO because the number of quality backlinks that your site has helps to back up the content quality on your site.

Backlinks play a very important role for end users and search engines. For search engines, they help them to figure out how relevant and authoritative your site is to your topic. Backlinks also send a signal to search engines that there are other sites who are endorsing your work. If there are a lot of sites that link to the same site or page, search engines learn that the content is worth sharing a link to, and as such, they rank the site higher on the results page. For a long time, the number of backlinks helped to show the popularity of a page, but today, we have different algorithms. These new algorithms were made to help determine other ranking factors. Pages will rank higher depending on the quality of the links that other sites are giving them instead of the quantity.

As for end-users, backlinks connect them with information that is close to what has been written by other sites. Backlinks work like a connection point for information that a reader may want to check out. It gives them a solid experience because it sends them directly to other desirable information.

While it is pretty much impossible to know the algorithm that is used by Google and other search engines to qualify content, there are some good ideas for site managers and owners to use to help improve their rankings and to create genuine backlinks.

What you can do is use the following tricks and tips in order to create backlinks without having to beg other people. These will help you to grow your online presence:

1. Let other bloggers credit the work they have done for you.

Everybody wants to create a portfolio in order to showcase their best work; whether they are business owners, entrepreneurs, copywriters, web designers and so on. Most of the time, these portfolios will also have some kind of backlink to other sites so that their viewers can review the work of their service provider.

Not only will allowing backlinks from portfolios help to improve the other person's business, but it will also place you higher within the search rankings for Google.

2. Talk to an influencer.

Using influencers as a marketing tactic is very popular right now. A lot of brands want to know how to get an athlete or celebrity to endorse their work, or become business partners with them. But you can do things a different way. You can choose to interview influencers in order to gain knowledge from them that could help your audience.

If you have yet to build connections to some influencers, you will need to be really good at email outreach and have good people skills. If you get the interview, it is very important to make sure that you have some thoughtful questions put together, and that you respect the person's time. Most people will want to keep the interview under 15 minutes, but if you know what you want to ask and have spent some time coming up with good questions, then you should be able to get plenty of insight during that time. Your interview can be published as a video or a transcript.

3. Create content that is shareable.

Shareable content is simple content that can be shared, which provides you with the chance to have your work shared throughout the internet and ups your odds of having your site linked to multiple platforms and web pages. Whether you choose to come up with well-researched blog posts, infographics, or actionable e-books, any content that is shared can be distributed through a call-to-action asking your readers to share the information any way they want to.

Pinterest, the often forgotten social media platform, is a great way to get backlinks. It's important that you make sure that your highly valuable content, infographics, case studies, and blog posts, are linked to a board on your Pinterest. If somebody finds your information helpful, there is a good chance that they will end up creating a backlink when they post the content on their website.

Your initial reach can easily be done through social media, hashtags, and other types of targeted distribution in order to get your work to others within your chosen niche.

4. Come up with a quiz.

Quizzes are very popular and they tend to be shared a lot. If you create a quiz for your site, you can embed it and get backlinks like you do when you have infographics. You need to make sure that your quizzes are fun. You don't have to make them be a knowledge test. It is a good idea to make quizzes that will encourage people to look inward and think about who they are; the result they get will then be something they want to share. This is something that Buzzfeed has capitalized on.

5. Use backlinks on your website.

Another way to make sure that you create shareable content is to create well-researched posts that link your readers to other important content within your niche. For example, you could come up with countdown posts to your top travel blogs so that you can link to other popular websites, and this creates an opportunity for that popular site to share your work and then create a link back to your site.

All of this means that you need to make sure you put your best foot forward when you are trying to generate backlinks, so it is important that you give shout-outs to the content creators, services, or products that make your life better.

You could also decide to do some sort of content round-up to bring together helpful tricks and tips for a specific concept or topic. If you want to do something like this, using Feedly can help you out. Feedly gives you the ability to find posts and articles that relate to certain topics. Coming up with a content round-up once a week will keep your readers updated on what they find important, and you should always link back to every website that you mention.

6. Share testimonials.

When you provide free testimonials, it is a win-win for everybody. The person you share a testimonial about gets free publicity and you also get your company and name shared on their site, as well as a backlink. Obviously, you should make sure that you are an actual customer of the company. You should never share a testimonial for a company or product you have never used.

7. Write guest posts for other sites.

Guest posts are at the top of the list for ways to showcase your expertise and generate backlinks. The majority of blogs and websites will have a short biography at the top or bottom of the posts, which will give you a space for a backlink.

Not only will doing these guest posts give you the chance to show off your knowledge, but working with other people will help you to build your professional rapport and create a brand personality. It can be hard to get up the nerve to reach out to other websites, but it is worth it if they do agree to post your guest post.

8. Do more online networking.

Whether you're a business owner or online entrepreneur, you have probably been informed more than once that networking is the key to business success. Networking has now made it to the digital realm using sites like Facebook and LinkedIn for business. Networking now has more benefits than ever before, with new opportunities to pitch guest posts, share content, and agree to add backlinks to sites of people who you have created a close professional relationship with.

Networking is great for everybody involved, and it gives you the chance to work on your professional communication abilities and business-building strategies.

9. Get more creative.

If you want to generate backlinks faster, then you need to get more creative. Having plenty of shareable content is a high-value, high-return endeavor, so why shouldn't you use some creativity in order to begin a new project to form some backlinks?

Using your various social media platforms to link to your site is extremely helpful, but this should be used sparingly. Don't link to your website with every single post. If you are an expert, then why shouldn't you share some of the work that you have done for other people? Reports and case studies about past work or customer experiences should and can be freely shared within your social media world, and it will demonstrate your value and expertise to future customers.

Much in the same way that you allow your digital service providers and designers to promote work they have done for you, you can also ask your clients to share what you have created for them. Case studies can also be very helpful when you want to land a guest post deal with a major website, as it lets them know that you care about what you are doing and are proud of it.

10. Collaborate with others on projects.

Using collaboration within a creative endeavor is always a great way to generate backlinks and to reach a larger audience. Things like podcasts have become more and more popular with business owners and creatives. This is because it gives them the chance to share their expertise while also linking back to their site in the episode description.

11. Make sure you stick to your niche.

Exchanging backlinks and networking can bring everybody immense rewards, but only if things are done correctly. You need to make sure that you take some time to get to know the other person, their business, and how your work can fit into their site. For example, you shouldn't worry about sharing in-depth case studies on coaching people on leadership development if direct ties don't exist.

It is important to stick with your niche when it comes to generating backlinks, so you need to make sure that your link sharing matches up with your niche so that you have a clean "record" because this will help with your rankings.

12. Get interviewed and perform interviews.

It doesn't matter what industry you are in, interviews are done regularly to create shareable content. If you are great at public speaking or you have the time to come up with a thoughtful reply to interview questions, this can help to improve your number of backlinks.

The main thing you need to remember when generating backlinks is making sure that each website that links to you is just as dedicated to sharing quality content as you are. While we are unsure of the criterion that classifies a site as "quality," it is very impressive what a few high-value backlinks are able to do with your rankings.

Trying to come up with backlinks is tedious, but if you are serious about your blogging and generating good backlinks on several accounts and websites within your niche, you will be able to stay high up in the ranks with Google and keep traffic coming to your site.

Remember that your content and website quality goes a long way in creating relationships and professional rapport with others who may backlink to your site. You want to make sure that your content is always actionable and useful; that it targets high-rated sites; and that you constantly nurture your online relationships to get the backlinks that will positively affect your rankings.

Proven Strategies: Google AdSense Earns This Blogger $800/Week

It might be all fine and dandy to hear how you can use AdSense to improve your blog and make it profitable, but it means nothing if you don't have proof to back it up. So that's what this last section is going to do. I'm going to share with you a true story about a man who was able to use Google AdSense to bring in around $800 each week.

This blogger receives most of his blog traffic from Facebook. He is a niche blogger, and one of his best days with Google AdSense made him close to $200. The main reason for this was because his post went viral on Facebook. According to him, 85% of his blog traffic comes from Facebook and the rest comes from email marketing.

While he does make a lot of money through Facebook itself, we are going to talk about how he also monetizes with Google AdSense. While Google doesn't bring in as much money as Facebook does, because it is pay per click, it does bring in quite a bit per week. In fact, it probably brings him more per week than most people's jobs pay them.

Google AdSense is one of the simplest things that you can start monetizing your website with. Even when you are only getting 1000 to 2000 people to your blog each day, it can still sometimes provide you with around $20 a day. Now, in this success story we're talking about, the blogger is driving traffic to his blog through email marketing, Facebook, and several other sources.

The way he ensures he makes his money through AdSense is to make sure that he focuses his traffic on the United States. The US tends to have more clicks on the ads and it has the highest pay rate. While many people say in order to be profitable with Google AdSense you have to rank high on Google, this blogger says that's not necessarily true. Ranking on Google can help you earn more revenue with AdSense, but according to the man in our example, as long as you have a good email list, you shouldn't have a problem with earning AdSense revenue.

To make sure that he makes the most money possible with AdSense and his other revenue options, he has blogs that require daily content. This means that he is sending things out to his followers every single day, which means that people are receiving updates from him every day. This ensures that nobody ever forgets about his site and there is somebody on the website each day.

For the blog, he shares news each day. This can be done in almost every niche. For example, if you have a sports blog, you can easily share news about UFC, or whatever sport you blog about. The man also explained that in order to get to where he is today, he had to invest a bit of money into driving traffic to his sites. He used Facebook ads, and by doing this, he was able to capture email addresses and subscribers. Then he could send them updates about new posts whenever he wanted.

This blogger believes the reason that he is so successful is that he has picked a niche that requires daily content. He explained that all other big blogs like Buzzfeed started out being run by a daily blogger. By making sure you have something to share every day that will drive high-quality traffic, then you are well on your way to succeeding. Daily news content that fits with your niche is one of the best ways to build up an audience quickly.

He also talks about how investing some money into his blog has helped him. He bought content and pays around $200 or more each month for a website hosting account that will ensure the site runs smoothly with a lot of traffic. He also spent $10 to $15 each day on posts to help drive traffic to the ads, but he said you don't have to do this; it's just what he chose to do. Once he got his audience up to 10,000 to 15,000 people, his audience started to grow by itself and he stopped having to pay for traffic.

The man ends his advice by saying that the $800 he makes each week with AdSense comes from two blogs that he has on one AdSense account.

But, throughout this blogger's whole story about how he makes upwards of $800 each week with AdSense, he kept saying that he monetized his sites in other ways as well. Relying solely on AdSense is not the best idea, because it requires clicks and it requires people to be on a PC. It doesn't work as well for mobile users. That said, you should still use AdSense. It is a great revenue option and will bring in more money.

Conclusion

Thank you for making it through to the end of *Blogging: Unlock the Secrets to Making Your Blog Posts into Profit and Discover How Bloggers Make Money Online Utilizing Affiliate Marketing and Other E-Commerce Skills for Passive Income*. It should have been informative and provided you with all of the tools you need to achieve your goals: whatever they may be.

The next step is to use the information you have learned within this book. While there may be a lot to it, the easiest place to start is with your niche. You can't start blogging until you know what you want to blog about. Figure out your niche and then start looking at what other people are doing in that area. Use that information to learn how you can make it better, and then move onto creating your blog. Once you feel comfortable with your blog and you have begun to post regularly and attracted some loyal readers, you can start to branch out in other ways, like e-commerce or creating informative products like an online class.

While you are doing all of this, you still need to remember to keep an eye on your analytics and use advertising. These are how you will make sure you keep your information in line with your competition and continue bringing in more and more readers. With the right approach, you can succeed and profit from your blog.

Finally, if you found this book useful in any way, a review on Amazon is always appreciated!

Printed in Great Britain
by Amazon

49524404R00125